The Principal As Instructional Leader

A Handbook for Supervisors

Sally J. Zepeda

EYE ON EDUCATION

6 DEPOT WAY WEST, SUITE 106

LARCHMONT, NY 10538

(914) 833–0551

(914) 833–0761 fax

www.eyeoneducation.com

Library of Congress Cataloging-in-Publication Data

Zepeda, Sally J., 1956–

  The principal as instructional leader : a handbook for supervisors /

Sally J. Zepeda.

       p.   cm.

Includes bibliographical references and index.
ISBN 1-930556-57-8

  1. School principals—United States—Handbooks, manuals, etc. 2. School supervision—United States—Handbooks, manuals, etc. 3. Educational leadership—United States—Handbooks, manuals, etc. I.

  Title.

  LB2831.92.Z46 2003

  371.2′012—dc21

                                                                                    2003043905

10 9 8 7 6 5 4 3

Editorial and production services provided by
Richard H. Adin Freelance Editorial Services
52 Oakwood Blvd., Poughkeepsie, NY 12603-4112
(845-471-3566)

Also Available from EYE ON EDUCATION

Instructional Supervision:
Applying Concepts and Tools
Sally J. Zepeda

101 "Answers" for New Teachers and Their Mentors:
Effective Teaching Tips for Daily Classroom Use
Annette L. Breaux

What Great Principals Do Differently:
15 Things That Matter Most
Todd Whitaker

The Call to Teacher Leadership
Sally J. Zepeda, R. Stewart Mayers, & Brad N. Benson

Staff Development: Practices That Promote
Leadership in Learning Communities
Sally J. Zepeda

Dealing with Difficult Teachers, Second Edition
Todd Whitaker

Motivating and Inspiring Teachers:
The Educator's Guide for Building Staff Morale
Whitaker, Whitaker, and Lumpa

Achievement Now!
How to Assure No Child is Left Behind
Dr. Donald J. Fielder

Coaching and Mentoring
First-year and Student Teachers
India J. Podsen and Vicki Denmark

Teaching Matters:
Motivating & Inspiring Yourself
Todd and Beth Whitaker

Teacher Retention:
What Is Your Weakest Link?
India J. Podsen

Differentiated Instruction:
A Guide for Elementary School Teachers
Amy Benjamin

Differentiated Instruction:
A Guide for Middle and High School Teachers
Amy Benjamin

Data Analysis for
Comprehensive Schoolwide Improvement
Victoria L. Bernhardt

The School Portfolio Toolkit:
A Planning, Implementation, and Evaluation
Guide for Continuous School Improvement
Victoria L. Bernhardt

Dropout Prevention Tools
Franklin P. Schargel

Strategies to Help Solve Our
School Dropout Problem
Frankln P. Schargel and Jay Smink

Navigating Comprehensive School Change:
A Guide for the Perplexed
Thomas G. Chenoweth and Robert B. Everhart

Dealing with Difficult Parents
Todd Whitaker and Douglas Fiore

The Confrontational Parent
Dr. Charles M. Jaksec III

Bouncing Back!
How Your School Can Succeed in the Face of Adversity
Patterson, Patterson, and Collins

Creating Connections for Better Schools
How Leaders Enhance School Culture
Douglas Fiore

Handbook on Teacher Portfolios for Evaluation
and Professional Development (Includes CD-ROM)
Pamela Tucker, James Stronge, and Christopher Gareis

Acknowledgments

Numerous colleagues read and reviewed this manuscript while it was in process, including Dr. Lea Arnau, Director of Staff Development in Gwinnett County, Georgia. This book is all the stronger because of the insights of the reviewers, all practicing administrators in K–12 schools, who included: Rebecca F. Harrison, Principal, Caprock High School, Texas; Deborah Jagoda, Principal, St. John's Lane Elementary School, Maryland; Elizabeth A. City, Principal, Kestrel Heights School, North Carolina; and Stephen M. Laub, Principal, Rolla Junior High School, Missouri.

A special thank-you goes to Dr. Helen Fish, who helped by looking over the keyboard while I double-checked references, and to Garrick Askew, a graduate assistant in the Program of Educational Leadership at the University of Georgia, who helped secure materials from the library.

As always, heartfelt appreciation goes to Bob Sickles for his belief in the work of principals as instructional leaders.

SJZ

About the Author

Sally J. Zepeda has served as a high school teacher, director of special programs, assistant principal, and principal before entering higher education. An associate professor and Graduate Coordinator in the Department of Educational Administration and Policy at the University of Georgia, she teaches instructional supervision and other courses related to professional development and the work of the principal. Dr. Zepeda has written widely about educational administration, supervision of teaching, and leadership. Her books include *Supervision of Instruction: Applying Tools and Concepts*; *The Call to Teacher Leadership* (with R. Stewart Mayers and Brad Benson); *Staff Development: Practices That Promote Leadership in Learning Communities*; *Supervision and Staff Development in the Block* (with R. Stewart Mayers); *The Reflective Supervisor: A Practical Guide for Educators* (with Raymond Calabrese); *Hands-on Leadership Tools for Principals* (with Raymond Calabrese and Gary Short); and *Special Programs in Regular Schools: Historical Foundations, Standards, and Contemporary Issues* (with Michael Langenbach).

What's on the CD and How to Use it!

The CD-ROM accompanying this book contains electronic versions of many of the forms, enabling you to fill them out, customize them, and save and print them using Microsoft Word.

Also available is an annotated list of web sites with useful information on action research, peer coaching, portfolio development, mentoring, induction, and other related topics.

To use the interactive forms, following the following instructions:

Complete the form by typing in the blanks provided and/or by clicking on the checkboxes. Use the **Tab** key to move from field to field. When you are finished, save the file with a unique name by using the **Save As** function.

Worksheets and forms are "protected", that is, the instructions on the form and its structure are locked and can not be changed unless you choose to do so. If you want to make modifications to the language on the form (such as inserting the name of your school or district, or otherwise customizing the language on the form) follow these directions:

(1) Choose **Unprotect Document** from the **Tools** menu.

(2) Type in the password, "Modify" (it must be typed exactly as shown here; it is case sensitive) and click the OK button. The form will unlock and become a regular Word document.

(3) Save the file to your hard drive with a new name using the **Save As** function.

While a document is unprotected, form functionality is unavailable. To re-enable form functions, choose Protect Document from the Tools menu. Note that re-enabling a form will remove any data that you previously inserted into the form fields.

The interactive forms available on this CD are listed here; the files are named by their book page number:

♦ Chapter 2. Vision, Mission and Culture

Page 27

Page 31

Page 46

◆ Instructions

◆ Useful Web Sites

Permission and Help

Permission is granted to reproduce these forms for educational purposes. This material may not be sold or repackaged without the written permission of the copyright holder and the publisher.

If you have any difficulty with the forms, please consult with your technology coordinator or network administrator. Eye On Education does not provide technical support.

Table of Contents

1

The Principal as Instructional Leader

In this Chapter ...

♦ Instructional leadership—what is it?
♦ Instructional leaders:
  • Make a commitment to learning
  • Provide connectivity and cohesion
  • Build strong teams of teacher leaders
  • Understand change
♦ Organization of the book

Very few people would disagree that the work of the principal is multifaceted, hectic, and fraught with uncertainties, and given the ongoing press for accountability, the very work of the principal as instructional leader is shifting to ensure "results." There are myriad day-to-day activities that take principals away from the important work of instructional leadership because these activities need administrative detail and attention to ensure the overall effective management of the school. However, no matter how important this "other" work is, Hoy and Hoy (2003) assert, "Schools are about teaching and learning; all other activities are secondary to these basic goals" (p. 1). *The Principal as Instructional Leader: A Handbook for Supervisors* examines the work that must be accomplished by principals as the instructional leaders of their schools. Very specifically, this book provides examination of learning and leading in the areas of developing a vision and culture that supports the supervision of the instructional program, staff development, and other processes to help teachers further develop their teaching.

The principal must be in a position to promote continuous learning and development of teachers who are challenged to teach students to higher standards of accountability. Tirozzi (2001) indicates, "The principals of *tomorrow's* schools must be instructional leaders who possess the requisite skills, capacities, and commitment to lead the accountability parade, not follow it" (p. 438, emphasis added). To accept this challenge, principals will need to be able to:

♦ Set the tone for their buildings;

♦ Facilitate the teaching and learning process;

♦ Provide leadership and direction to their schools' instructional programs and policies;

♦ Spend significantly more time evaluating staff and mentoring new teachers;

♦ Sustain professional development for themselves and their staff members; and

♦ Nurture personalized school environments for all students. (p. 438)

Tomorrow is too late. Principals must be able to lead in the present because school systems will always look to their principals for direction, guidance, and the commitment to make learning for teachers and students a top priority.

What gets in the way of principals paying full attention to the work of instructional leadership? Responses from principals in the field include a range of responses *from* attending to student discipline, intervening with angry parents, and completing paperwork and reports needed by central office *to* complying with special education rules and regulations, administering the testing program, tracking the results of standardized testing, and seeing to the maintenance of the physical plant. Principals are the stewards of their buildings overseeing the operations of the school—the instructional program, the budget, the facilities, the discipline program, the community outreach efforts—the list never ends.

The principal does not need to walk alone. Many principals have the assistance of assistant principals, lead teachers, department chairs, grade-level leaders, and others who help to ensure the orderly operations of the school. However, some principals do not have full- or part-time assistance from school personnel assigned to work alongside the principal. Regardless of the configuration of personnel who assist the principal, the final responsibility for the success of the instructional program and its people—teachers and students—rests squarely on the shoulders of the principal, and this is a sobering proposition. It is no wonder that there is a pending shortage of principals and a trend for assistant principals not to desire the move up to the principal's office.

There is a need for optimism for those who are in or aspire to the position of principal, and there is a need to elevate the work of the principal as instructional leader. The instructional leadership of the principal is worth the effort and worthy of a recommitment of those who lead in concert with teachers toward improvement and effectiveness. The guiding premises needed to achieve improvement and effectiveness are embedded in the day-to-day work of the principal, and these premises are probably rooted in the reasons why an individual sought and accepted the position of principal.

Instructional Leadership—What Is It?

Deriving the meaning of the term *instructional leadership* is elusive. The construct of instructional leadership is a complex one that has been written about and researched from the perspective of the work of those in the position of the principal (Sergiovanni, 1987, 1995), the traits and characteristics of principals (Yukl, 1994), school effectiveness (Edmonds, 1979; Purkey & Smith, 1983), change (Murphy, 1994a), and school improvement (Murphy, 1992, 1994b). Included in this search for meaning have been numerous movements (transformative leadership, shared decision making), preparation standards for principals (Interstate School Leaders Licensure Consortium [ISLLC], 1996), the call for moral leadership (Sergiovanni, 1995), the development of learning communities (Barth, 2001a; Sergiovanni, 1994; Lambert, 1995), the need for an ethic of care (Barth, 2001a; Noddings, 1992), and so goes the list.

Leadership that focuses on instruction has a strong purpose and an equally strong commitment to student learning. The Wisconsin Department of Public Instruction (DPI) (2002) provides a construct for instructional leadership—purposes, key ideas, and the leadership needed by the principal who wears the mantle of instructional leader. Figure 1.1 (pp. 4–5) details these ideas.

What Is the Work of the Principal as Instructional Leader?

In an era of increased demands for accountability, the work of the principal as the instructional leader is under debate by many scholars, and the work of the principal as leader *in practice* is often at odds with the research reported. Instructional leadership is easy to see but difficult to define. The elusive nature of defining leaderships is caused, in part, to the specific nature of the context of the school, the characteristics of the student body and personnel, the climate of the school, the culture and norms of the school, the communication patterns, and the values that the school holds as its own.

Make a Commitment to Learning

In 1999, the U.S. Department of Education (along with others) hosted a two-day summit composed of nationally known superintendents and principals. In the U.S. *Policy Brief* (1999), the participants reported that principals as instructional leaders devote:

Text continues on page 5.

Figure 1.1. Defining Instructional
Leadership Needed by the Principal

Instructional Leadership Defined

Strong leadership promotes excellence and equity in education and entails projecting, promoting, and holding steadfast to the vision; garnering and allocating resources; communicating progress; and supporting the people, programs, services, and activities implemented to achieve the school's vision.

Rationale for Leadership

Effective leadership is essential to the development and continuing improvement of any organization. An educational leader is needed to focus efforts on excellence and equity.

Key Ideas

1. Leadership roles are assumed by a variety of persons in addition to principals and superintendents, including teachers, parents, students, and community leaders.

2. Leaders demonstrate knowledge, respect, and responsiveness to the diverse cultures, contributions, and experiences that are part of the school and society.

3. School leaders expect and hold staff accountable for challenging all students with a rigorous, culturally relevant curriculum and for demonstrating high expectations for each student.

4. School leaders ensure that each school has financial, material, and programmatic resources adequate to provide each student an equitable opportunity to learn.

Successful Schools Have Leadership That

1. Demonstrates flexibility in dealing with change and a willingness to experiment.

2. Makes decisions based on attaining the most positive results for students, rather than on adhering to or maintaining an established system.

3. Analyzes disaggregated data from multiple sources and uses it to inform decisions.

4. Uses technology effectively to lessen the load of routine tasks and to provide more effective communications.

5. Recognizes individual differences in staff and students and provides opportunities to meet their needs.

6. Facilitates and builds consensus that guides rather than mandates.

7. Uses a blend of top-down and bottom-up decision-making processes.

8. Inspires, persuades, and influences others by their own actions and attitudes.

9. Stays current on educational research and trends and provides the same information to stakeholders.

10. Responds to the needs of culturally and linguistically diverse students and their families.

11. Maintains a focus on the possibilities and opportunities instead of the barriers.

12. Cultivates support for the school and its mission among all segments of the community, school board, district personnel, and other concerned individuals and groups.

Source: *Characteristics of Successful Schools—Leadership* (2002). Wisconsin Department of Public Instruction. http://www.dpi.state.wi.us/dpi/dlsea/sit/cssldrshp1.html Used with permission.

the bulk of their time, energy, and talents to improving the quality of teaching and learning. Leaders . . . have a deep understanding of teaching and learning, including new teaching methods that emphasize problem solving and student construction of knowledge. Good instructional leaders have a strong commitment to success for all students, and are especially committed to improving instruction for groups of students who are not learning now. (¶ 2)

In an early synthesis of instructional leadership, De Bevoise (1984) indicates that instructional leadership includes "those actions that a principal takes, or delegates to others, to promote growth in student learning" (p. 15). Similarly, Sergiovanni (1987) asserts, "successful leadership … within the principalship is directed toward the improvement of teaching and learning" (p. 7).

Leadership That Transforms

A careful reading of the transformational leadership literature reveals two distinct concepts of transformation. One values leadership that transforms organizations, and views people as instrumental to achieving the organizational vision. The other focuses on the primary value of transforming people as individuals, as followers, and as team members. The latter approach honors individual talent development, relationships, collaborative systems, and shared vision, seeking the empowerment of individuals as well as work teams in pursuit of the broader vision. (Komives, 1994, p. 49)

Provide Connectivity and Cohesion

Instructional leaders seek to transform learning for both students and the adults who teach children, and they do this not alone but through the very people of the school. Principals who are instructional leaders "link" the work of leadership and learning to everyone in the school. Figure 1.2 (p. 7) illustrates "The Concepts: Types of Work" and the absolute necessity of the principal linking this work to the development of a learning community.

Figure 1.2 illustrates the cyclical and interconnected aspects of work. Figure 1.3 (p. 8) further defines the various types of work needed to connect the work of the principal in leading learning and school improvement.

Effective leaders provide *cohesion* among the work needed to build an instructional program that links the vision and mission of the school to

- ♦ supervising instruction;
- ♦ evaluating teachers;
- ♦ providing staff development and other learning opportunities for teachers;
- ♦ promoting a climate of instructional excellence; and
- ♦ establishing collegial relationships with teachers.

Cohesion is built on more than linking the work of instructional leadership and the management of tasks. A more powerful force—relationships with others—builds cohesion, and this "connective leadership" is what will help to bind people and their values to the work they do. Komives (1994) credits Lipman-Bluemen (1989) with coining the term *connective leadership*, and she reports that connective leaders (a) link people with each other, forming communities and

Figure 1.2. The Concepts: Types of Work

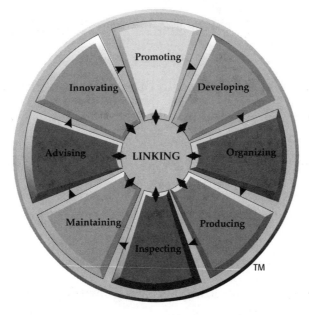

Source:[1] The Concepts: Types of Work, accessed September 21, 2002, from http://www. tms.com.au/ tms06.html, Team Management Systems © Prado Systems Limited 1993, 2002. Used with permission.

teams that work effectively together; and (b) link people with goals, ideas, and visions built from their shared dreams (p. 50).

Connectivity promotes the ability of the instructional leader to focus squarely on learning while simultaneously leading school personnel. Effective instructional leaders are able to master first and then transcend the technical aspects of management so that they can:

♦ Lead schools in a way that places student and adult learning at the center.

♦ Set high expectations and standards for the academic and social development of all students and the performance of adults.

♦ Demand content and instruction that ensure student achievement of agreed-upon academic standards.

---

[1] Team Management Systems © Prado Systems Limited 1993, 2002. All references to Team Management Systems copyrighted materials are reproduced by special permission of Team Management Systems. This copyrighted material may not be reproduced by any means without the written permission of Team Management Systems, 1041 Sterling Road, Ste 101, Herndon, VA 20170, USA. All rights reserved.

Figure 1.3. Defining Work

Advising	Gathering and reporting information
Innovating	Creating and experimenting with ideas
Promoting	Exploring and presenting opportunities
Developing	Assessing and testing the applicability of new approaches
Organizing	Establishing and implementing ways of making things work
Producing	Concluding and delivering outputs
Inspecting	Controlling and auditing the working of systems
Maintaining	Upholding and safeguarding standards and processes
Linking	Coordinating and integrating the work of others

Source:[2] The Concepts: Types of Work accessed September 21, 2002, from http://www.tms.com.au/ tms06.html, Team Management Systems © Prado Systems Limited 1993, 2002. Used with Permission.

♦ Create a culture of continuous learning for adults tied to student learning and other school goals.

♦ Use multiple sources of data as diagnostic tools to assess, identify, and apply instructional improvement.

♦ Actively engage the community to create shared responsibility for student and school success. (National Association of Elementary School Principals, 2001)

---

[2] Team Management Systems © Prado Systems Limited 1993, 2002. All references to Team Management Systems copyrighted materials are reproduced by special permission of Team Management Systems. This copyrighted material may not be reproduced by any means without the written permission of Team Management Systems, 1041 Sterling Road, Ste 101, Herndon, VA 20170, USA. All rights reserved.

Build Strong Teams of Teacher Leaders

Given the complexities of schools, leadership cannot be vested solely to the principal, and as the saying goes, *No man stands alone.* Principals assert their effectiveness by diffusing leadership to a larger set of stakeholders, namely, teachers. Diffusing leadership is much different from delegating work and duties just to get things done or to lighten the workload. Diffusing leadership entails trust, collaboration, support, and advocacy for extending the boundaries of authority beyond the position and the person who holds the title of principal. Effective principals not only support the construct of teacher leadership, but they also support and actively engage team development as a way to engage more teachers in school leadership.

There is a strong correlation between leadership and learning for students and teachers: "Indeed, if schools are going to become places in which all children are learning, all teachers *must* lead" (Barth, 2001b, p. 444, emphasis in the original). Teacher leaders promote learning when they lead, and this is why principals must find opportunities for teachers to be involved in leadership within the school and beyond. Short and Greer (1997) describe the skills of principals who promote leadership:

- Build trust;
- Communicate more openly;
- Promote risk-taking;
- Engage in open problem-solving; and
- Build a commitment and support for change. (p. 183)

These are the essential skills that principals need to promote teacher leadership that goes beyond "getting work done" in the school. Effective instructional leaders are able to frame teacher leadership within the context of the school, and they are able to value teachers as leaders who can:

- Develop the instructional program.
- Make positive changes in the school.
- Share their expertise with others.
- Shape the culture of the school.

Teacher leaders who actively work within the realm of the instructional program make significant contributions to other related areas beyond their individual classrooms.

Principals who support teacher leadership opportunities do more than work with groups—they cultivate capacity for leadership among many teachers, who in turn, promote leadership among more teachers. The next logical step in promoting leadership that is iterative (Lieberman & Miller, 1999) is to work at developing teams of teacher leaders. Team structures are ideally suited to promote teacher leadership because in teams:

- Leadership is rotated among members.

- Team members are interdependent—they are accountable to each other on an equal playing field.

- Decisions are made collaboratively among team members, and this increases the commitment to the work of the team.

- The team upholds a purpose, a set of goals, and a vision for the work of the team.

- The team structure promotes participative meetings and collective work that is shared equally and equitably among team members.

People working together for the common good, if nurtured, can yield many positive results—reduced isolation, the generation and refinement of ideas and approaches, and synergy from working with others who, if the conditions are right, may agree and disagree with one another. Wheatley (n. d.) offers several pervasive reasons for leaders to affirm the possibilities of teams. Leaders who encourage teachers to work beyond their own individual causes are *Life Affirming Leaders*, who:

- Know they cannot lead alone. No one person is smart enough to know what to do.

- Have more faith in people than they do in themselves, and patiently and courageously insist on their participation.

- Recognize human diversity as a gift, and the human spirit as a blessing.

- Know that people only support what they create and will only act responsibly for things they care about.

- Solve unsolvable problems by bringing new voices into the room.

- Continually expand who's included in decision making.

- Convene and host conversations that really matter.

- Know that trust and caring make everything possible.

- Offer meaningful work as the greatest motivator.

- Freely express gratitude, appreciation, and love.
  http://www.fromthefourdirections.org/tpl/ourarticles.tpl

The development of teams provides cohesion to the achievement of the school's mission, and more importantly, Harvey and Drolet (1994, p. 1) indicate, "Structures and organizations are made great by their people infrastructure. Capable, creative, positive, thoughtful people are the fundamental building blocks of strong, surviving organizations."

Understand Change

School systems respond to change daily in response to both internal forces (e.g., changes in the learning needs of students) and to external forces (e.g., increasing accountability standards). It is the principal's role to set forth the conditions necessary for teachers to implement change because change is integral to school improvement processes. "School cultures are incredibly resistant to change. This is precisely why school improvement—from within or from without—is usually so futile," are the words of Barth (2001a, p. 8), who despite the anguish involved in change, believes that schools can rise to the occasion and make the changes necessary to improve learning and leading. Effective instructional leaders understand that the difficulty of change rests in the nature of human response to change:

> Change leads a doubly double life. There is a fundamental duality to our response to change: we both embrace and resist it. We acknowledge its inevitability, and yet a profound conservative impulse governs our psychology, making us naturally resistant to change and leaving us chronically ambivalent when confronted with innovation. (Evans, 1996, p. 21)

For instructional leaders to assist teachers with the many challenges associated with meeting the needs of students and the school, an understanding of change is necessary. Figure 1.4 (p. 12) provides a broad overview of assumptions about change and leadership.

Change in one area typically signals that change is necessary in others (e.g., Fullan, 2001; Lewin, 1936; Sarason, 1995), and this is true because schools are composed of interconnected parts. For change to be successful, principals need to involve teachers as leaders. Schools wanting to improve will need to change patterns of thinking, cultures entrenched by past practices, and the climate in which the school's culture rests. Top-down leadership that mandates change meets resistance.

Figure 1.4. Assumptions about Change Related to Leadership

Assumptions about Change (CBAM) (Hord, Rutherford, Huling-Austin, & Hall, 1987)	*Leadership Needed by the Principal (Calabrese, 2002)*	*Leadership Translated to Action*
◆ Change is a process, not an event.	◆ Leaders meet the needs of their constituents.	◆ Involving teachers as leaders;
◆ Change is accomplished by individuals.	◆ Leaders create a sense of personal urgency for change among members of the organization.	◆ Supporting improvement through supervision and evaluation procedures that are responsive to teacher needs;
◆ Change is a highly personal experience.	◆ Leaders sustain change by learning to manage the pace of change.	◆ Creating and maintaining an environment conducive to innovation and risk taking;
◆ Change involves development growth.	◆ Effective change leaders construct a climate that encourages organizational members to gain a personal understanding of their status and weigh that understanding against the potential for improvement.	◆ Providing ongoing staff development to support teacher and administrative learning;
◆ Change is best understood in operational terms.		◆ Facilitating open and honest communication about innovations; and
◆ The focus of facilitation should be on individuals, and the context (pp. 5–6).	◆ The leader constructs a psychologically safe environment in which members are free to question their beliefs and values without the risk of threat or embarrassment (pp. 11–15).	◆ Securing necessary resources for supporting change.

Source: Calabrese; 2002; Hord, Rutherford, Huling-Austin, & Hall, 1987.

Organization of the Book

Instructional leadership is difficult to define, but instructional leaders are about the business of making schools effective by focusing their attention, energy, and efforts toward student learning and achievement by supporting the work of teachers. To accomplish this critically important work, principals who want to be instructional leaders need to be able to delve into the parts that make the whole of working with teachers to improve their instructional practices. The chapters in this book examine

- Vision, Mission, and Culture (Chapter 2)
- The Connection between Supervision, Staff Development, and Teacher Evaluation (Chapter 3)
- Informal and Formal Classroom Observations (Chapter 4)
- Pre-Observation Conferences (Chapter 5)
- Extended Classroom Observations and Data Collection Instruments (Chapter 6)
- The Post-Observation Conference (Chapter 7)
- Final Thoughts (Chapter 8)

For ease in using this book as a handbook for instructional leadership, the content of each chapter is highlighted. Within each chapter, research and concepts are highlighted, but more importantly, suggestions for implementation along with the tools to apply research into practice are provided.

Instructional Leaders Build a Vision of Possibilities to Create Collaborative Cultures

Quality teaching and knowledge about instruction should be a part of the vision for student achievement. Instructional leadership involves knowing what good teaching is and how good teaching leads to student learning. Building a vision for student success and instructional leadership is an ongoing reflective process, and building the vision among the members of the school community is an iterative process that begins with the instructional leader looking *within* for the core values and beliefs that motivate her to act on these values and beliefs. The effective principal also looks to the school community to engage all stakeholders in developing the vision. The vision drives all actions and allocation of resources. Instructional leaders protect the vision, leading people toward the end goal.

Culture is a defining point for the school and what occurs—when, how, under what circumstances, why, and in some instances, why not. The culture of the school encompasses the values, norms, and traditions that have evolved over time (Deal & Peterson, 1993, 1999). Schein (1992) reports that certain actions of the leader act as "embedding mechanisms" that can serve to perpetuate or to change a school's culture. Embedding mechanisms, according to Schein include such items as:

♦ What leaders pay attention to, measure, and control on a regular basis;

♦ How leaders react to critical incidents and organizational crises;

♦ Observed criteria by which leaders allocate scarce resources;

♦ Deliberate role modeling, teaching, and coaching;

♦ Observed criteria by which leaders allocate rewards and status;

♦ Observed criteria by which leaders recruit, select, promote, retire, and excommunicate organizational members. (p. 231)

Instructional Leaders Connect Staff Development and Teacher Evaluation as Seamless Practices

All schools have structures to support teachers—supervision, staff development, and teacher evaluation. However, many school leaders fail to connect these support structures to create seamless learning opportunities for teachers. For professional development to make a difference in the lives of teachers, and by extension the lives of students, there is a need for multiple learning opportunities bundled for teachers to work in concert with each other. The defining features of such efforts include opportunities embedded in the workday (job-embedded learning), replete with opportunities for reflection, dialogue, and collaboration. Without a school culture that supports collaboration, the efforts of the principal will yield few lasting results. Without collaboration, learning communities cannot develop. In schools that are learning communities, teachers "constantly search for new ways of making improvements" (Fullan, 2001, p. 60), and this is why teachers must be provided ongoing support and encouragement to make changes in their instructional practices.

Effective instructional leaders recognize there is a relationship between accountability, improved teaching, and support that teachers need from administrators who oversee the instructional program. Accountability systems have essentially created a ripple effect between what students and teachers do. Recognizing this effect, the National Association of Elementary School Principals (NAESP) reports:

We've learned that it's meaningless to set high expectations for student performance unless we also set high expectations for the performance of adults. We know that if we are going to improve learning, we must also improve teaching. And we must improve the environment in which teaching and learning occurs. (2001, p. 2)

What makes it difficult to connect activities designed for professional learning? Here are a few possibilities to consider:

- Teacher evaluations must be completed by a certain date, usually in the spring, two or more months before the end of the year.

- A prescribed number of classroom observations must be completed before a summative rating is assigned, but this number can be as few as one. Moreover, in some states the length of time mandated for observing a teacher is as little as 15 minutes per observation.

- Teachers leave the building to attend staff development seminars throughout the year but have no opportunities to share with others what they have learned. Moreover, follow-up is sparse, perpetuating staff development as "shotgun learning."

- Central administrators often book big-name consultants to address district-wide issues on teacher workdays, but follow-up activities cease when the consultant leaves.

- Mentoring and induction efforts delivered by central office personnel do not necessarily reflect the context of the school; site and district-level activities typically stress more global issues, while building-level programs stress more context-specific issues.

- The efforts of mentors are not factored into the equation of what supervisors do to assist beginning teachers or other teachers.

- Supervisors often focus their attention on the hot spots—a single grade level implementing a new program, or deficit areas (grade levels that have performed poorly on standardized tests). (Zepeda, 2003)

Support systems include supervision, staff development, and other measures such as peer coaching, study groups, and mentoring. Moreover, these supports need to address immediate and long-term needs and must provide a unity of purpose to ensure coherence.

Instructional Leaders Conduct Informal and Formal Classroom Observations

Effective principals are visible, and they make the time to visit classrooms both informally and formally to lend support, give encouragement, and to assess the overall instructional program. Because of their presence, leaders have credibility with their teachers. Findings reported in the U.S. *Policy Brief* (1999) indicate that effective

> Principals know how to evaluate instruction and give frank, powerful feedback that encourages teachers to teach better and students to learn more. These principals engage the whole school in continuous dialogue about what good teaching looks like and whether students are doing quality work. (¶ 3)

It is difficult to understand the complexities of teaching without having familiarity with students and teachers as instruction unfolds in classrooms. In schools where instructional supervision unfolds in the main office, teachers miss learning opportunities. Effective principals get instructional supervision out of the main office, and they frequent classrooms.

Instructional Leaders Conduct Pre-Observation Conferences before Formal Classroom Observations

With the premise that supervision cannot occur in the principal's office and that principals need to conduct both informal and formal classroom observations, it is critical to look at what contributes to more effective formal classroom observations. One of the most essential aspects of a formal classroom observation is a quality pre-observation conference where the teacher and principal engage in discussion about teaching and learning. It is during the pre-observation conference that the teacher identifies a focus area for an upcoming classroom observation. The focus guides the principal in knowing what tool to use to collect data that will be shared with the teacher in the post-observation conference. The focus is an area that the teacher seeks to explore through the assistance of the principal who will collect data pertaining to the focus.

Instructional leaders understand the composition of the students in classrooms, they can see how teachers change gears to meet student needs, and they have an eye for examining the connection between what a teacher does and then what students are able to do because of instruction. Instructional leaders are able to talk with their teachers and engage in intensive discussion about learning and instruction. It is difficult to achieve these goals when principals do not engage teachers in discussion, and the pre-observation conference is where the dialogue about teaching and learning begins. There can be no substitutes.

Instructional Leaders Use a Variety of Tools to Collect Stable Data during Classroom Observations

With the focus established in the pre-observation conference, the principal enters the classroom with certain tools that will assist in collecting data related to that focus. There are a variety of tools the principal can use to record the both the teacher's and student's words and actions. Familiarity and practice with data collection tools ensures that more stable data are collected. Data are important because data serve as the basis for the discussion in the post-observation conference.

Instructional Leaders Conduct Post-Observation Conferences after Formal Classroom Observations

After conducting the extended classroom observation, the post-observation conference provides the opportunity for the teacher and principal to engage in discussion related to the focus established in the pre-observation conference. Data inform this discussion, and data serve as a means for the teacher to "see" an aspect of teaching. Teachers want feedback, and they desire the opportunity to talk about teaching and the impact of instruction on students. For adults, Brookfield (1986) believes that "learning [is] further enhanced by regular feedback on progress, and positive feedback will act as a reinforcer for the pursuit of more learning" (p. 29). Brookfield (1995) also indicates that feedback needs to be followed by purposeful reflection on practice, and that reflection is a "uniquely adult form of learning" (p. 222). The supervision literature stresses the importance of dialogue to promote growth and development (Glickman, Gordon, & Ross-Gordon, 1998), to enhance sense making (Zepeda, 2000), and to foster the interchange of ideas between professionals (Waite, 1995).

Chapter Summary

Instructional leadership is an elusive concept; however, effective principals engage in work that supports teachers in improving their instructional practices, and this type of support occurs in classrooms, not the principal's office. Instructional leadership is not a spectator sport. Effective principals are instructional leaders because they make a commitment to learning, and they connect the work of improved student learning and teaching by building strong teams of teacher leaders.

It is essential for the principal to understand change, particularly why people resist change. Understanding change is important for the principal who strives to work with teachers improve their instructional practices. As a supervisor, the principal is engaged in helping teachers examine their instructional practices—what is working, what is not working, and how modifications can be made given the characteristics of students.

To supervise effectively, principals formally and informally supervise teachers, and they have a command of the tools involved in conducting classroom observations and supporting the talk about teaching that occurs before and after classroom observations. Moreover, the principal as supervisor is able to link supervision, staff development, and teacher evaluation as seamless processes while providing differentiated support through such activities as peer coaching and action research.

Suggested Reading

Building Teams

Dyer, W. G. (1995). *Team building: Current issues and new alternatives* (3rd ed.). Reading, MA: Addison Wesley.

Harvey, T. R., & Drolet, B. (1994). *Building teams, building people: Expanding the fifth resource.* Lancaster, PA: Technomic.

Katzenbach, J. R., & Smith, D. K. (1993). *The wisdom of teams: Creating the high performance organization.* Boston, MA: Harvard Business School Press.

Maeroff, G. I. (1993). *Team building for school change: Equipping teachers for new roles.* New York: Teachers College Press.

Change

Calabrese, R. L. (2002). *The leadership assignment: Creating change.* Boston, MA: Allyn and Bacon.

Chance, P. L., & Chance, E. W. (2002). *Introduction to educational leadership and organizational behavior: Theory into practice.* Larchmont, NY: Eye on Education.

Chenoweth, T. G., & Everhart, R. B. (2002). *Navigating comprehensive school change: A guide for the perplexed.* Larchmont, NY: Eye on Education.

Conner, D. R. (1993). *Managing at the speed of change: How resilient managers succeed and prosper where others fail.* New York: Villard Books.

Principal Leadership

Crow, G. M., Matthews, L. J., & McCleary, L. E. (1996). *Leadership: A relevant and realistic role for principals.* Larchmont, NY: Eye on Education.

Fielder, D. J. (2003). *Achievement now! How to assure no child is left behind.* Larchmont, NY: Eye on Education.

Kouzes, J. M., & Posner, B. Z. (2001). *The leadership challenge: How to keep getting extraordinary things done in organizations* (3rd ed.). San Francisco, CA: Jossey-Bass.

Short, R., & Greer, J. (1997). *Leadership for empowered schools.* Columbus, OH: Merrill.

Teacher Leadership

Katzenbach, J. R., & Smith, D. K. (1993). *The wisdom of teams: Creating the high performance organization.* Boston, MA: Harvard Business School Press.

Katzenmeyer, M., & Moller, G. (1996). *Awakening the sleeping giant: Leadership development for teachers.* Newbury Park, CA: Corwin Press.

Lieberman, A., & Miller, L. (1999). *Teachers—Transforming their world and their work.* New York: Teachers College Press.

Zepeda, S. J., Mayers, R. S., & Benson, B. N. (2003). *The call to teacher leadership.* Larchmont, NY: Eye on Education.

2

Vision, Mission, and Culture

Instructional Leaders Build a Vision of Possibilities and a Collaborative Culture

In this Chapter …

♦ The school vision—beginning the journey

♦ School mission—charting the course

♦ Vision, mission, and action—connecting the pieces

♦ Vision and mission thrive in healthy cultures

Regardless of position, effective leaders are able to create a vision of possibilities within the organization (Krug, 1992), and according to Barth (2001a), "There is no more important work … than helping create and then employing an inspiring, useful vision" (p. 194). The vision guides, gives direction, brings comfort and stability in times of rapid change, and inspires people to connect to the work needed to improve learning for both students and teachers.

Creating a vision is more than a product; creating the vision is a multifaceted process that requires careful attention to such areas as values, beliefs, and the school culture. There is interplay between school culture and climate in the development of building the vision and mission of the school. As instructional leader, the principal must understand the complexities of the school's culture as it "reflects what organizational members care about, what they are willing to spend time doing, what and how they celebrate, and what they talk about" (Robbins & Alvy, 1995, p. 23). Therefore, the discussion of establishing a collaborative culture to support the vision and mission will be explored throughout this chapter with examples of leading the school through the process of developing a vision and mission by examining the values and beliefs of the members of the school.

The School Vision—
Beginning the Journey

What is a Vision and
Why is the Vision Important?

A vision is encompassing. Embedded in the vision and by extension the school culture are the beliefs, values, purposes, and goals that when bundled serve as a means to focus the work of the school. Conley (1996) believes the vision acts as an *internal compass,* and Speck (1999) makes a compelling argument that "Vision is what separates the principals who are school leaders from those who are simply managers" (p. 117). Principals who are leaders embrace the opportunity for leading in the development of a vision because the vision is a powerful commitment to the future of the school. The vision makes important statements about what values, beliefs, and ideals the organization embraces about learning, teaching, and relationships.

There are standards in place for the preparation of school leaders most notably by the Interstate School Leaders Licensure Consortium (ISLLC). Although these standards are primarily for the preparation of school administrators, they are important for practicing administrators to have knowledge and understanding. For now, attention is given to the language of Standard 1 (Fig. 2.1) because this standard relates to the encompassing nature of the school vision.

Figure 2.1. ISLLC Standard 1

Standard 1   A school administrator is an educational leader who promotes the success of all students by facilitating the development, articulation, implementation, and stewardship of a vision of learning that is shared and supported by the school community.

Source: Interstate School Leaders Licensure Consortium, 1996. *Standards for School Leaders.* http://www.ccsso.org/standrds.html.

Within this standard (as in others), ISLLC calls for leaders to have a knowledge base, a set of dispositions, and the ability to perform certain tasks to get the important work needed to ensure student learning is accomplished. The performance aspects, *what leaders are able to do,* are perhaps, more important than the knowledge; however, it is difficult to "do" without "knowing." Figure 2.2 (p. 24) illustrates the performance or the "do" statements used to show what effective instructional leaders are able to do *with the vision.*

Vision is embedded in everything a leader does, and the vision serves to:

♦ Unify people within the school and its many communities;

♦ Focus people on the future and point to what the school wants to become;

♦ Promote growth by providing the means for people to stretch while facing the challenges associated with reaching the vision.

♦ Empower the organization and its people to hold beliefs and values about schooling—the work of teachers, students, and the opportunities each has for developing.

A school's vision is the lifeline of the school, and an effective vision is a powerful reminder of what the school and its people are committed to achieving. Figure 2.3 (p. 25) offers an overview of the characteristics of an effective school vision.

Although all members of the school build an effective vision, the leadership of the principal is an absolute necessity. The principal will be called to uphold the values in which the vision rests and to focus and refocus all efforts and resources to this end.

Leadership and the Vision

Instructional leadership emanates from within the individual, and Krug (1992) asserts "what distinguishes effective instructional leaders from others is not a distinctive set of characteristics but an approach to their work that is guided by a distinctive set of beliefs about what is possible" (p. 441). Effective instructional leaders are able to look within to identify core beliefs that define beliefs about teaching and learning.

(Text continues on page 26.)

Figure 2.2. Performance Aspects of
ISLLC Standards Related to Vision

Performances (what effective leaders are able to do)

The administrator facilitates processes and engages in activities ensuring that:

♦ The *vision* and *mission* of the school are effectively communicated to staff, parents, students, and community members.

♦ The *vision and mission* are communicated through the use of symbols, ceremonies, stories, and similar activities.

♦ The core *beliefs* of the school vision are modeled for all stakeholders.

♦ The *vision* is developed with and among stakeholders.

♦ The contributions of school community members to the realization of the *vision* are recognized and celebrated.

♦ The progress toward the *vision and mission* is communicated to all stakeholders.

♦ The school community is involved in school improvement efforts.

♦ The *vision* shapes the educational programs, plans, and actions.

♦ An implementation plan is developed in which objectives and strategies to achieve the *vision* and goals are clearly articulated.

♦ Assessment data related to student learning are used to develop the school *vision* and goals.

♦ Relevant demographic data pertaining to students and their families are used in developing the school *mission* and goals.

♦ Barriers to achieving the *vision* are identified, clarified, and addressed.

♦ Needed resources are sought and obtained to support the implementation of the school *mission* and goals.

♦ Existing resources are used in support of the school *vision* and goals.

♦ The *vision, mission,* and implementation plans are regularly monitored, evaluated, and revised.

Source: Interstate School Leaders Licensure Consortium, 1996. *Standards for School Leaders*. Council of Chief State School Officers. http://www.ccsso.org/standrds.html.

Figure 2.3. Characteristics of an Effective School Vision

A vision must inspire.	A vision that inspires moves people out of their heads and into their hearts. Once members allow the vision to live in their hearts, they freely give of their time, energy, and emotion to the vision.
A vision challenges all members of the organization.	A vision issues a challenge to members and motivates them to aspire to reach for something beyond their grasp. A vision fosters solidarity, solidifies relationships, and boosts morale.
A vision stands the test of time.	A vision over arches the membership—it is the constant from one generation of teachers and students to the next.
A vision is evolutionary.	A vision is a living entity, one that is subject to the laws of life and death. If it is a growing, life producing entity, it will constantly adapt to the future. Visions that do not adapt soon die.
A vision guides members during times of chaos.	During turbulent times, schools that lack an effective vision drift aimlessly and are swept in any number of ways by the currents until they are finally beached on the shore or submerged.
A vision empowers.	An effective vision empowers its members who can act individually and creatively because every action, decision, and solution is directed toward achieving its mission.
A vision exists in the future.	A vision does not live in the past—it is future oriented.

Source: Adapted from Calabrese, Short, & Zepeda, 1996. Used with Permission.

Effective Leaders Listen to their Own Voice

Building a vision for student success and improved instruction is an ongoing, reflective, and iterative process that begins with the instructional leader looking *within* for the core values and beliefs that motivate her to act on these values and beliefs. As a starting point, reflect on your current leadership position and identify what you stand for as a leader. The following questions can guide this process.

♦ What do I stand for?

♦ What is my personal vision about teaching, students, and achievement?

♦ What does good teaching look like? What separates good teaching from excellent teaching, mediocre teaching?

♦ What types of support would teachers need to achieve good teaching as I envision this picture of good teaching?

♦ What types of teaching do students need in order to learn? Can all children learn?

Seikaly (2002) offers an exercise (Figure 2.4) that can help in the identification of core values.

The values of the principal are central to the development of an environment that supports learning. Values motivate and give direction: They focus the principal on what is important and why. According to Seikaly (2002), values shape what principals do as leaders. The principal can further clarify values by answering key questions, including:

♦ What does the principal plan for?

♦ What does the principal monitor?

♦ What does the principal model?

♦ What does the principal reinforce through recognition and celebration?

♦ What behavior is the principal willing to confront?
  (http://www.mdk12.org/process/leading/principals_role.html)

With an awareness of their own values and beliefs, principals will be in a better position to hear the voices of others.

Figure 2.4. Exercise for Identifying Core Values

Questions to Ask	*Tracking Responses*
1. School should teach ...	
2. A good school is one that ...	
3. A successful student is able to ...	
4. An effective classroom is one in which ...	
5. A good school / central office staff member (i.e., teacher, principal, supervisor) is one who ...	
6. An effective school faculty/central office division is one that ...	
7. A quality instructional program includes ...	

Source: Seikaly, 2002. Exercise for Identifying Core Beliefs. http://www.mdk12.org/process/leading/core_beliefs.html. Used with Permission.

Effective Leaders Listen to the Voices of Others—They Look Throughout the School

A vision is not static. Leaders who empower others as "leaders" within the context of the school encourage and purposefully seek out opportunities for community members to create and recreate the vision to fit the needs of the school (Komives, 1994). Effective leaders invite and encourage a broad base of participation in determining and developing the vision by first asking the right questions and then hearing the answers. Some questions to ask teachers, students, and parents include:

- ♦ What does good teaching look like?
- ♦ What are the qualities of good teaching?
- ♦ How is good teaching supported?
- ♦ What gets in the way of teachers being able to be effective instructional leaders within their classrooms?

The principal who hears the answers to these questions is able to bring action to what is heard. Kouzes and Posner (2001) in their book, *The Leadership Challenge: How to Get Extraordinary Things Done in Organizations,* offer an inclusive and empowering set of practices that can serve as a framework for the principal's actions. Principals send a clear message of commitment to acting on what is heard when they:

- **Challenge the process** *by* searching for opportunities and experimenting and taking risks.

- **Inspire a shared vision** *by* envisioning the future and enlisting others in the development, implementation, and assessment of the vision.

- **Enable others to act** *by* fostering collaboration and strengthening others.

- **Model the way** *by* setting the example and planning small gains along the way.

- **Encourage the heart** *by* valuing others, recognizing the contributions that individuals make, and celebrating accomplishments (Kouzes & Posner, 2001).

Looking Throughout requires that the principal commit to finding the time for teachers, staff, parents, and students to have the opportunity to shape the vision because "vision making hardly lends itself to tidy resolution during a two-hour faculty meeting" (Barth, 2001a, p. 197). Because "vision making" is at the core of developing a vision that will become the living document of the school, it is suggested that the principal consider:

- Finding the resources to take the faculty on a one or two day retreat during the summer.

- Using plan time (one or two days) before the school year begins to get teachers and others framing the vision.

- Committing time throughout the school year—release days for inservice and faculty meeting times for teachers to have sustained time to identify their values and beliefs.

Finding and using time to include others is important because a vision will only encompass the learning community when the ideas and values of everyone are heard. However, time is sometimes a constraint, given unions, contract agreements, and limitations in the discretionary authority of the principal to obtain funding for release time. The principal will need to scan the environment, seeking opportunities to work within these limitations.

A principal can include faculty, staff, parents, students, and others in the process of developing the mission in two complementary ways. One way is to refer to Figure 2.4 (p. 27) and have faculty in small and large groups come to consensus on what they believe about schools, students, and the process of education within the structure of the school. Faculty can track, prioritize, and target beliefs and values that are most pressing to acknowledge in the work needed to provide a sound educational program.

A set of beliefs might resemble the ones developed by principal Jeff Powers and the teachers at the Dassel-Cokato Middle School in Cokato, Minnesota.

Beliefs of the Dassel-Cokato Middle School Teachers and Administrators

We believe the Dassel-Cokato Middle School should:

- Meet the unique needs of early adolescents.
- Be child centered.
- Reflect the values and priorities of the community, parents, and students.
- Provide students the opportunity to explore a wide variety of interests and skills.
- Offer many opportunities for students to be successful physically, socially, emotionally, and intellectually.
- Recognize and reward their successes.
- Encourage individual differences and attempt to meet unique student needs.
- Develop in students a respect for themselves and others.
- Develop in students a sense of interdependence and belonging.
- Emphasize academically challenging experiences that fosters thinking, problem solving and develop an attitude for life-long learning.
- Emphasize an allied arts curriculum that stimulates creativity, enjoyment, and knowledge.

Source: Dassel-Cokato Middle School. Cokato, Minnesota.
http://www.dc.k12.mn.us/MSCHOOL/Default.htm. Used with Permission.

A second way to engage the learning community in the building of a vision is to examine the overall landscape of the school, assessing "where we are now." Assessing the current situation can be an instructive exercise for the school community, and the information discovered can assist to:

- Open lines of communication by including those closest to learning in the process.

- Identify possible needs and barriers to developing a schoolwide vision and mission.

- Provide a baseline of data to track shifts in values, beliefs, and needs throughout the years.

- Chart progress in getting closer to the ideals with which the vision is built.

The work of identifying core values, beliefs, and ideals makes more sense to the specific context of the school, the characteristics of the students and faculty, and the culture of the school. Bruce Hammonds (2002) of At leading-learning. co.nz (http://www.leading-learning.co.nz/school-vision/assess-school.html) developed an assessment (Figure 2.5, p. 31) as a means of assembling baseline information, and this instrument can be used throughout the year to track this information.

The use of an assessment (see Figure 2.5, p. 31) makes sense for several reasons. This assessment can help teachers and others know where they fit in and how they can enhance the school and its programs, and it can serve to break barriers by getting people to share their perspectives of where things stand. In addition, this type of assessment can serve as a way to track how people, programs, beliefs, and values centering on the vision evolve over time. The principal could use this assessment periodically throughout the year by asking teachers to self-rate where they are across each one of the nine areas and anonymously to turn in their assessments. The results can then serve as a way to promote ongoing discussion.

Developing the Vision is Ongoing

A vision is brought to life with members of the learning community involved in "purposeful tinkering" (Hong, 1996) by revisiting and refining the vision through intensive and frequent discussion, ongoing reflection, fault-free experimentation, and constant evaluation on efforts and effects of the vision on changes in practice. Purposeful tinkering creates the opportunity for the vision to be examined and modifications made while reaching for the vision.

Figure 2.5. Assessing the School

1. Does the school have a shared vision and values, a mission that unites all. Is there a deep understanding of the mission by all?

    0 ←——————————→ 10

2. Does the school have a shared set of common practices and beliefs that effectively expresses the values and mission statement that meets the needs of all?

    0 ←——————————→ 10

3. Does the school have a realistic, shared, well-defined strategy plan that effectively expresses the vision, mission, and shared beliefs?

    0 ←——————————→ 10

4. Is there alignment between each member and the mission statement/values and shared beliefs that reinforces the strategy plan? Do you all work as a team to achieve the mission?

    0 ←——————————→ 10

5. Does the school have a management style that is congruent with the mission and shared values, or is it inconsistent or lacking?

    0 ←——————————→ 10

6. As an individual, do you have the skills and style to make a full contribution to the vision, mission of the school?

    0 ←——————————→ 10

7. Do you communicate well between each other, share concerns, strategies, co-operate, and work in teams to achieve the mission?

    0 ←——————————→ 10

8. Do you know or trust each other enough to really be a high performance team?

    0 ←——————————→ 10

9. Do you believe you are able to do what you believe in; that you have personal integrity?

    0 ←——————————→ 10

Analyze the results and use as a comparison after a vision has been defined.

Source: Hammonds, 2002. Involving the Learning Community in Developing the Vision http://www.leading-learning.co.nz/school-vision/assess-school.html. Used with Permission of Bruce Hammonds and At leading-learning.co.nz.

A Vision Is Only as Strong as Its Culture

Because of the interrelated nature of values, beliefs, assumptions, and norms, it is almost impossible to speak of school vision and mission without examining school culture because, according to Stolp and Smith (1995), "the culture tells people in the school what is truly important and how they are to act" (p. 14). According to Peterson (2002):

> School culture is the set of norms, values and beliefs, rituals and ceremonies, symbols and stories that make up the "persona" of the school. These unwritten expectations build up over time as teachers, administrators, parents, and students work together, solve problems, deal with challenges and, at times, cope with failures. (p. 10)

Leonard (2002) indicates that positive cultures are marked by professional collaboration that is "evidenced when teachers and administrators, share their knowledge, contribute ideas, and develop plans for the purpose of achieving educational and organizational goals" (¶ 4). In healthy school cultures, principals work with teachers; they have a shared vision and mission; they focus on student learning; and they work under a common set of assumptions about learning for both students and adults. A positive culture is *aligned* to goals and objectives that are consistent with the vision and the mission of the school.

A healthy culture does not magically occur. Strong cultures emerge, in part, by the efforts of the principal, and there is nothing more visible than the work of the principal. What the principal and the members of the administrative team emphasize, reward, and sanction comes to symbolize publicly what is important. Fiore (2001) believes that there are key behaviors of principals in schools that reinforce healthy or unhealthy cultures (Figure 2.6, p. 33).

School Mission—Charting the Course

Related to the vision is the school mission. The mission is the totality of the vision. A recent headline, "Lack of Mission Hurting Schools" (Nathan, 2002, *Pioneer Press*—Minnesota) is a sober reminder that every school needs a mission.

The mission is the purpose on which all efforts of the school focus attention. A mission and its statements serve to focus a school more explicitly on the meaning of the vision that include the beliefs and values of the school community. The mission helps guide the principal to focus, develop, and coordinate the various activities and programs found within the school.

Covey (1990) indicates that a mission statement "has the potential of being a living constitution—something that embodies deeply held values and is based on timeless principles" (pp. 185–186). Although most mission statements are

Figure 2.6. Principal Behaviors—Healthy and Unhealthy Cultures

Principals in Healthy Cultures ...	*Principals in Unhealthy Cultures ...*
♦ Are visible to all stakeholders	♦ Are rarely seen outside their office
♦ Communicate regularly and purposefully	♦ Find little time for communication
♦ Never forget that they are role models	♦ Feel that other people are responsible for their school building's physical needs—they take passive roles in decorating and furnishing their schools
♦ Are passionate about their work	
♦ Accept responsibility for the school's culture	
♦ Are organized	♦ See themselves as the lone leader, or "boss" of the school; they never empower teachers to lead
♦ Exhibit a positive outlook	
♦ Take pride in the physical environment of the school	♦ Are poorly organized
♦ Empower others appropriately	♦ Habitually make excuses for their school's shortcomings, blaming inadequacies on outside influences
♦ Demonstrate stewardship—they protect their school and its people.	

Source: Fiore, 2001. Principal Behaviors—Healthy and Unhealthy Cultures. Used with Permission.

relatively short (about 100 words or so), a school's mission statement is powerful. Fielder (2003) summarizes that a mission statement must be limited in scope, and further writes:

> It must clearly tell everyone including the uninformed reader what the organization is all about. It must be unambiguous in defining central purposes of the organization. It must contain phrases or words that mean the same thing to everyone so that there is no confusion about the organization's direction. (p. 1)

Fielder identifies four reasons why a mission needs to be purposefully *limited* in scope because:

1. It concentrates everyone's attention, energy, and efforts on accomplishing the mission. There are no activities, although enjoyable and even important, that do not lead to the mission.

2. When the mission is clear, it is much more likely that the mission will be accomplished.

3. It focuses resources into areas where they will be the most effective.

4. A limited mission provides a means by which everyone can measure the progress toward the mission. (pp. 3–5)

What comes first, the vision or the mission? The answer is neither, because the mission and the vision work in tandem. It is unlikely that a school will have one without the other. The vision is more elusive and often resides in the minds of the people, whereas the mission is visible in faculty handbooks and parent newsletters.

Values and Beliefs Serve to Link Vision and Mission

Embedded in both the school's mission and vision are values and beliefs. Given the primacy of values and beliefs, it is important to examine further the development of values and their subsequent statements. McNamara (1999) offers a series of insights about values and the subsequent statements leading to the development of a mission statement. Figure 2.7 offers the insights in the process of developing a value statement. The reader is cued to numbers 3 and 4 within Figure 2.7 as possible activities to assist with uncovering and prioritizing values. From such an activity, the principal is in a better position to know which values are in operation, which are prioritized over others, and which are lacking within the structure of the school.

Similar to the vision, the development of the mission is a process, and Covey (1990) believes that the "process of creating a mission statement is much more important that the actual document" (p. 185). Because nearly every school has a mission statement, the principal needs to have knowledge about the existing mission. This is especially true if the principal is new to the school. If a newcomer, the principal needs to understand the complexities of the mission statement and its history. The following questions can guide the principal in better understanding the school's mission.

Figure 2.7. Developing a Values Statement

1. Values represent the core priorities in the organization's culture, including what drives members' priorities and how they truly act in the organization, etc. Values are increasingly important in strategic planning. They often drive the intent and direction for "organic" planners.

2. Developing a values statement can be quick culture-specific, i.e., participants may use methods ranging from highly analytical and rational to highly creative and divergent, e.g., focused discussions, divergent experiences around daydreams, sharing stories, etc. Therefore, visit with the participants how they might like to arrive at description of their organizational values.

3. Establish four to six core values from which the organization would like to operate. Consider values of customers, shareholders, employees and the community.

4. Notice any differences between the organization's preferred values and its true values (the values actually reflected by members' behaviors in the organization). Record each preferred value on a flash card, and then have each member "rank" the values with 1, 2, or 3 in terms of the priority needed by the organization with 3 indicating the value is very important to the organization and 1 is least important. Then go through the cards again to rank how people think the values are actually being enacted in the organization with 3 indicating the values are fully enacted and 1 indicating the value is hardly reflected at all. Then address discrepancies where a value is highly preferred (ranked with a 3), but hardly enacted (ranked with a 1).

5. Incorporate into the strategic plan, actions to align actual behavior with preferred behaviors.

Source: McNamara, 1999. Developing a Values Statement. http://www.mapnp.org/library/ plan_dec/str_plan/stmnts.htm. Used with Permission.

Examining the Mission Statement

- ♦ Who was involved in the development of the site-level mission statement?

- ♦ When was this mission statement developed?

- ♦ What was the process used to develop the mission statement?

- ♦ When was the last time the mission statement was formally examined? Modified?

- ♦ What evidence exists that teachers, parents, and students know and understand the mission statement?

After examining the history of the mission statement, attention needs to turn to fact-finding to see how the mission statement is used as a means to forward all programs within the school.

Time to Fact-find about the Mission Statement

- ♦ What artifacts point to the school mission statement?

- ♦ How is the mission statement used to examine instructional practices, curriculum development, student assessment procedures, and other practices in the school?

Developing a Mission Statement

The mission statement is where the proverbial "rubber meets the road," and the mission statement helps to answer fundamental questions such as:

- ♦ Who are we as a collective faculty and school?
- ♦ What do we want to strive to become?
- ♦ Whom do we serve?
- ♦ What are the needs of those we serve?
- ♦ What are our strengths and weaknesses?
- ♦ Where are we headed?
- ♦ How will we know when we have arrived?

McNamara (1999) offers some ideas that can assist with developing a mission statement (Figure 2.8).

Figure 2.8. Developing a Mission Statement

1. Values represent the core priorities in the organization's culture, including what drives members' priorities and how they truly act in the organization, etc. Values are increasingly important in strategic planning. They often drive the intent and direction for "organic" planners.

2. Developing a values statement can be quick culture-specific, i.e., participants may use methods ranging from highly analytical and rational to highly creative and divergent, e.g., focused discussions, divergent experiences around daydreams, sharing stories, etc. Therefore, visit with the participants how they might like to arrive at description of their organizational values.

3. Establish four to six core values from which the organization would like to operate. Consider values of customers, shareholders, employees and the community.

4. Notice any differences between the organization's preferred values and its true values (the values actually reflected by members' behaviors in the organization). Record each preferred value on a flash card, and then have each member "rank" the values with 1, 2, or 3 in terms of the priority needed by the organization with 3 indicating the value is very important to the organization and 1 is least important. Then go through the cards again to rank how people think the values are actually being enacted in the organization with 3 indicating the values are fully enacted and 1 indicating the value is hardly reflected at all. Then address discrepancies where a value is highly preferred (ranked with a 3), but hardly enacted (ranked with a 1).

5. Incorporate into the strategic plan, actions to align actual behavior with preferred behaviors.

The Development of the Mission Embraces Inclusiveness

Developing an effective mission statement is a process that takes time, a commitment to inclusiveness, and an eye for accepting ambiguity throughout the process. Without inclusion, the mission statement will quickly be forgotten because the mission lives only in the mind of the principal and not in the collective minds of teachers and others of the learning community.

An inclusive process will help members to build and to further clarify their beliefs and values while learning skills such as how to suspend judgment and how to frame ideas, as well as witnessing first-hand how a collection of people become a group committed to a common cause—the mission of the school. The following strategy is offered as one way to develop a mission statement.

Strategy for Developing a Mission Statement

- After examining the vision and the values that are embedded in the vision, ask each teacher to develop a DRAFT mission statement for the school.

- Form smaller groups of teachers (four members per group) and ask the members of the smaller groups to share their mission statements with one another. Ask members to note similar themes from the four statements and meld the four statements into a single mission statement.

- Convene the smaller groups, and in front of the faculty, have each team present its mission statement.

- Solicit two volunteers to list on butcher-block paper (have these volunteers positioned in the back of the room) the common ideals across groups. Solicit two volunteers to track outliers—not-so-common ideals. (The intent is to capture what the community values.)

- When all groups have finished sharing their mission statements, have the two volunteers present to the larger group the "commonalities" across the mission statements. Include the two volunteers who have tracked the outlier ideals and have this team present those ideals.

- Ask the faculty to return to their groups and rank order the top two or three commonalities. Ask each group to report their commonalities on an index card. Collect the index cards and have two volunteers tally the rank orderings and report the results to the larger group.

♦ Seek consensus from the faculty on the top three or four ideals—these ideals will serve as the basis for the writing of the mission statement.

♦ Depending on the size of the faculty (and the number of teams of four), have each group appoint a member from the team to serve on a larger committee to draft the school's mission statement.

♦ Convene this group to develop the draft of the mission statement.

♦ Once the draft is developed, distribute the mission statement and ask teachers to reflect on the mission statement.

The principal can distribute the draft of the mission statement to parents, students, the central office, and to the larger community in which the school resides. The objective is to solicit feedback and to get stakeholders involved in the work of the school. Many schools have homepages and enhanced means to communicate with stakeholders, including e-mail, a district television station, and electronic newsletters. Meetings with the school's parent groups, external constituents (Chamber of Commerce and school-business partners) are also sources the principal can turn to for input as the mission statement develops.

A few thoughts on the wording of a mission statement ...

The Peter F. Drucker Foundation for Nonprofit Management offer several criteria for an effective mission statement. An effective mission statement:

♦ Is short and sharply focused

♦ Is clear and easily understood

♦ Defines why we do what we do; why the organization exists

♦ Does not prescribe means

♦ Is sufficiently broad

♦ Provides direction for doing the right things

♦ Addresses our opportunities

♦ Matches our competence

♦ Inspires our commitment

♦ Says what, in the end, we want to be remembered for

After a sufficient time has been given for reflection and feedback, the principal needs to reconvene the faculty to refine the mission statement. Teachers should be asked to respond with comments and questions to the draft mission statement. The principal can appoint a member or two of the committee that wrote the first draft of the mission statement to facilitate this meeting. The principal who hands over a meeting is essentially empowering others. Once agreement has been reached on the mission statement, the mission needs to be shared, celebrated, and then followed with a course of action to make the mission a living document.

Make a Big Deal Out of the Mission ...

- Print the mission statement on every formal document generated by the school.

- Celebrate the mission by hosting a "signing" party where faculty signs the mission statement. Follow up by having the mission statement printed on a tee shirt with teacher's signatures under the mission statement. Designate a day of the week and special occasions where teachers will be encouraged to "wear the mission."

- Post a copy of the mission statement in every classroom. Ask teachers to discuss the mission statement with their students.

- Include the mission statement on the school homepage, as a signature line on your e-mail, and on the district television channel.

- Develop a recognition program centering on the mission statement where students and faculty are recognized and honored for typifying the school mission in both big and small acts.

- Post the mission statement in the trophy case and have a "larger than life" poster with the mission at the main entrance of the school.

- Review the mission with every person who interviews for a position.

Vision, Mission, and Action—
Connecting the Pieces

A mission without action *diminishes* the effort extended to create it. The following strategy can assist bringing action to the mission.

Strategy for Developing an Action Plan to Launch the School's Mission

The action plan to meet the mission should span a short period—three to five years. Objectives that are specific, achievable, and measurable should be developed; otherwise, people will not be able to track results. Lunenburg (1995) suggests that goals should be:

- **Specific:** Goals are *specific* when they are clearly stated.

- **Measurable:** *Measurable* goals are precise and can be measured over time.

- **Achievable:** Goals are *achievable* if they are realistic. The effort needed to reach a goal can inspire greater effort; unrealistic goals are self-defeating.

- **Relevant:** Goals are *relevant* if they are viewed as important to the individual and to the group. Superficial goals are forgotten because they lack meaning.

- **Trackable:** Goals need to be *trackable* to check progress. Goals should not be so numerous or complex that they confuse rather than direct people.

- **Ongoing:** Not all goals will be completed by the end of a specified period. Some goals are achieved over a longer time; others can be reached more quickly.

Consider this objective: *The school will become more nurturing to students.* This objective is not specific, achievable, or measurable. At the end of three years, people will not be able to say whether the objective was met. A more focused objective reads, *The school will develop a program to focus on building the self-esteem of students.* The objective is specific, achievable, and measurable.

To get the process of developing an action plan started, the following ideas are offered with the reminder that each school is context specific; therefore, the principal should adapt these strategies to fit the needs of the school and to move closer to the mark of achieving the mission. This process takes time, and it is suggested that the principal slate either a full day or half-day to this process and a few follow-up sessions during scheduled faculty meetings. If this amount of time is not an available option, then the principal is encouraged to slate several faculty meetings to the work of developing the action plan. Depending on the configuration of the school (elementary, middle, high school), the principal can ask teams of teachers to work on generating ideas during team, grade, or subject plan time.

Time for Individual Reflection

♦ At a half-day retreat (or at a faculty meeting), give each teacher an index card, a sheet of paper with the mission statement, and a small scrap of paper with a number written on it. (A strategy to ensure that when teachers break out into smaller groups they work with people they do not usually work with daily (grade or team-level members) is to pass out numbers at random to the teachers or to have the teachers pick numbers out of a hat, and then form groups based on the numbers.) Ask each teacher to list the six most important things that they believe must be done in the next three years to implement the mission statement. After 10 minutes, ask each teacher to cross out one item from this list. This strategy helps people to start the thinking needed to prioritize items.

Moving into Small Groups of Four

♦ Ask teachers to form into groups by the number given to them (try to keep the group size to no more than four—this, of course, depends on the size of your faculty).

♦ Ask teachers to share their list of five most important things with each other and to note similarities and differences. Ask the group to come to consensus and develop a list of four (eliminating one item from the group list) most important objectives that are essential to fulfilling the mission. Then ask each group to prioritize this list (eliminating an item if they see a need).

♦ Suggested time: 30 minutes.

Merging Smaller Groups— Narrowing the Number of Objectives

To continue the process of coming to consensus and narrowing the objectives, merge two groups of four into a larger group of eight.

♦ Ask this larger group to share their objectives, noting commonalities and differences, and ask this group to narrow the number of objectives to three or four. Ask a member of this larger group to be prepared to share the objectives that they agree.

♦ Suggested time: 30 to 40 minutes.

Moving Back to the Larger Group

♦ Convene groups and have each group list their objectives.

♦ Solicit two volunteers to list on butcher-block paper (have these volunteers positioned in the back of the room) the common objectives across groups. These two volunteers will filter the objectives, eliminating "repeats" or ideas that are very similar. The principal or a member of the administrative team can assist with this filtering.

♦ When all groups have finished sharing their objectives, have the two volunteers present the commonalities across groups (ensuring that the objectives are written on the butcher block paper).

♦ Tape the butcher block sheets on walls, and let the whole faculty view the narrowed list of objectives (ask teachers to walk up to the sheets and mark up the sheets, tweaking words, phrases, etc. on the objectives.)

♦ Suggested time: Open-ended. This aspect of the process cannot be rushed. Depending on the time available, this might be the time to come to closure and return to this part of the process on another day.

Narrowing from *X* Number of Objectives to the Top Three Objectives—Time to Prioritize

Objectives must be manageable. Too many objectives, and the faculty will more than likely not be able to meet the mark (the intent and focus of the mission); too few objectives, and the faculty will not feel challenged.

♦ With the list of objectives written on the butcher block paper, ask the faculty members to review each objective and in their own minds prioritize the most important three objectives the school should focus to achieve the mission. After a few minutes, ask faculty to mill around the paper and put 1, 2, and 3 after their top three objectives. To ease with presenting the objectives, have faculty mark their priorities, and then tally their picks. The following can help to portray information.

Objective	Priority Number Given	Tally
We will begin an after-school program for reluctant readers and their parents.	1, 3, 1, 2, 3, 1	1 = 3
		2 = 1
		3 = 2
We will spend 15 minutes a day reading out-loud to our students.	1, 1, 1, 1, 1, 1, 3, 1, 2, 3, 1, 1, 2, 3, 1, 1, 1, 1, 3, 1, 1, 2	1 = 15
		2 = 3
		3 = 4

♦ Appoint or ask a volunteer to tabulate in rank order the numbers assigned to the priorities. If there is a tie, modify the process and have teachers rank the tie (with a 1 or a 2). This should break a tie.

Tip

Keep a log of all the objectives. Although some objectives might not have been ranked 1, 2, or 3, they are important and somehow might shed light on an area in need of attention.

♦ Review the top three objectives to ensure faculty agreement on the wording. Solicit any changes in the wording needed to make the objectives more clear.

♦ After the meeting, write the objectives after the mission statement.

Mission Statement
XXXXX

Objectives of the Mission Statement

1.

2.

3.

These objectives will assist the principal and teachers to focus more intently on achieving the mission. The objectives serve as a powerful reminder to what the principal and teachers need to focus the resources, time, and energy to achieve the mission. With the school mission and the objectives for meeting the mission, the principal is in a position to develop an action plan to include what is needed to achieve what the faculty thinks is most important for meeting the needs of the school and its people.

The Work of the Principal— Linking Vision, Mission, Objectives, and Strategies

The real work of the principal begins after agreement on vision, mission, and objectives bring these often elusive concepts into focus. To help the principal plan work and chart progress, Figure 2.9 (p. 46) can assist with keeping work moving forward by unifying vision, mission, objectives, and strategies.

The work of the principal in promoting the vision and mission is dependent on the ability to keep the ideals, values, and beliefs alive in the minds, hearts, and work of teachers and others. Persistence is needed, and Calabrese, Short, and Zepeda (1996) present several ways in which the principal keeps the focus on the mission.

Principals keep the mission alive by ...

♦ Continuously articulating the mission.

♦ Continuously referring to the mission.

♦ Continuously tying the mission to the vision.

♦ Continuously calling forth heroic efforts of the members to attain the goals identified in the mission.

♦ Recognizing the "warriors" who have committed themselves to the cause.

♦ Making the mission all consuming, so that the mission becomes the school culture.

Figure 2.9. Unifying Vision, Mission, Objectives, and Strategies

Vision and Mission	Objectives	Strategies
Vision We believe children can learn and all students deserve an educational foundation of basic skills that can build on strengths. **Mission** We are committed to the well-being and development of children, and we recognize, respect, and value the uniqueness of children. We are committed to providing a safe, nurturing, and stimulating environment in which children will have opportunities to realize their intellectual, physical, creative, and social/emotional potentials. We are committed to life-long learning, self-sufficiency and critical thinking. We are committed to helping children develop into responsible citizens who value diversity, are respectful of themselves and others, and the local and global worlds in which they interact. We maintain high academic expectations, and we promote strong school/home/community partnerships.	♦ To develop a research-based curriculum within and between grade levels so each student has the opportunity to meet or exceed standards at his/her highest individual potential in the areas of math, science, and English. ♦ To develop a schoolwide literacy program across the curriculum. ♦ To provide a secure and nurturing school environment that is aesthetically pleasing and functional. ♦ To promote an atmosphere of cultural appreciation, understanding, and cooperation within the community.	♦ Implement a balanced literacy program in all classrooms. ♦ Provide activities that accommodate hands-on learning and multiple intelligences. ♦ Provide opportunities for professional development at grade level and across grade levels. ♦ Implement school adopted curriculum and materials, supplementing as needed. ♦ Continue and improve governance system to ensure shared responsibility. ♦ Provide needed support systems to new teachers. ♦ Foster open communication between parents and teachers to promote mutual understanding of competencies and expectations. ♦ Raise school community awareness by identifying and acknowledging the school population.

Vision and Mission Thrive in Healthy Cultures that Build Collaboration and Trust

The leadership of the principal is critically important to building and sustaining the vision and mission. Part of this building process is sustaining a healthy culture, and there are two norms that principals can promote—collaboration and trust. The efforts of the principal to promote collaboration and trust must be pervasive. Shortcuts will dilute the efforts and signal insincerity to a commitment for the vision of what schools need s they strive to promote teacher growth and development as well as student achievement.

Building Collaborative School Cultures

Healthy school cultures thrive in environments built through collaboration, trust, and care for the members of the school. School culture can never be built through the sole efforts of the principal, and Lane (1992) believes:

> The culture-building mode is not meant to imply that the principal single-handedly constructs the school culture. Rather, it is meant to describe the principal's efforts to influence or shape the existing values and norms of the culture in a direction that best supports instructional effectiveness. (p. 92)

Kruse, Louis, and Bryk (1994) assert that collaborative school cultures are dependent on:

- *Critical elements of school communities*: reflective dialogue, deprivatization of practice, collective focus on student learning, collaboration, and shared norms and values.

- *Structural conditions*: time to meet and talk, physical proximity, interdependent teaching roles, communications structures, and teacher empowerment.

- *Social and human factors*: openness to improvement, trust and respect, supportive leadership, and socialization of teachers. (pp. 4–5)

The principal is in a position to support the development of each of these conditions through a variety of means that range from shared decision making, to implementing peer-coaching programs, and from supporting beginning teachers through formal and informal mentoring programs to providing time for teachers to meet.

Building a collaborative school culture and positive school climate are dependent on several variables, including, most notably, norms and workplace conditions. Norms and workplace conditions are interrelated, and together they form both the culture and climate of the school.

Norms

Norms are unwritten rules of behavior that serve as a guide to the way people interact with one another (Chance & Chance, 2002). Saphier and King (1985) identify 12 norms of school culture, which, if strong, contribute to the instructional effectiveness of a school. The norms that "grow" a strong school culture and climate include:

1. *Collegiality*: How people interact with one another, the openness members of the community have toward one another.

2. *Experimentation*: Risk-taking.

3. *High expectations*: Do people have high expectations for themselves, for each other, and for students?

4. *Trust and confidence*: Do people trust one another?

5. *Tangible support*: Resources—time, support.

6. *Reaching out to the knowledge bases*: Information is available.

7. *Appreciation and recognition*: People feel important, respected, and part of the school. They feel that what they do is important, and their colleagues, the administrators, and the larger community hold the work they accomplish in high esteem.

8. *Caring, celebration and humor*: People thrive when they feel emotionally supported. Communities take the time to celebrate—the big and small accomplishments of each other and students.

9. *Involvement in decision making*: Decision making spans the school environment and is not just a function of the administration.

10. *Protection of what is important*: Principals and others identify what is important and then protect time and secure resources to support priorities.

11. *Traditions*: Traditions shape the culture and traditions are upheld as part of the community.

12. *Honest, open communication*: People talk to one another; they share ideas openly without fear.

Collegiality and Collaboration

Principals dedicated to fostering the conditions for improved instruction promote collegial and collaborative relationships among teachers. The school climate dictates whether or not teachers collaborate with one another and whether or not interactions are collegial and inviting. Collaboration in schools has been marked as the "key schooling process variable for increasing the norms of student achievement" (Lunenburg, 1995, p. 41). Similarly, Hargreaves (1997) reports:

> Cultures of collaboration among teachers seem to produce greater willingness to take risks, to learn from mistakes, and share successful strategies with colleagues that lead to teachers having positive senses of their own efficiency, beliefs that their children can learn, and improved outcomes. (p. 68)

An important aspect of understanding the culture of a school is to know the faculty and the types of learning opportunities available to them vis-à-vis staff development, supervision, leadership opportunities, workplace conditions, and the relationships that teachers have with each other and the administration. Figure 2.10 (p. 50) can serve as a checklist for the principal to reflect about the programs for teachers that shape the school culture by proving opportunities for learning and leadership opportunities for teachers.

How can a principal promote the authentic norms of collegiality in which teachers take ownership in their interactions with each other? Interactions among teachers would be nestled in an environment that supports:

- *Interaction and participation.* People have many opportunities and reasons to come together in deliberation, association, and action.

- *Interdependence.* These associations and actions both promote and depend on mutual needs and commitments.

- *Shared interests and beliefs.* People share perspectives, values, understandings, and commitment to common purposes.

- *Concern for individual and minority views.* Individual differences are embraced through critical reflection and mechanisms for dissent and lead to growth through the new perspectives they foster.

- *Meaningful relationships.* Interactions reflect a commitment to caring, sustaining relationships. (Westheimer, 1998, p. 17, emphasis in the original)

Collaboration is about altering relationships and is dependent on the feeling of interdependence (*we are in this together*) and opportunity. When teachers collaborate, they share ideas and problem-solve solutions to the thorny issues they face in the classroom.

Figure 2.10. Programs for Teachers that Shape the School Culture

Programs for Teachers

♦ What types of professional development activities are available for teachers?

♦ How many teachers participate in these activities?

♦ What types of programs would teachers like to see initiated?

♦ Are teachers provided time during the day to observe each other teach and talk about what they learn from one another?

♦ What types of leadership activities are available for teachers?

♦ How many teachers are involved in formal and informal leadership activities?

♦ What types of teacher recognition programs are in place?

Sources: Adapted from Calabrese, Short, & Zepeda, 1996. Used with permission.

Professional Development ...

♦ Focuses on teachers as central to student learning, yet includes all members of the school community;

♦ Focuses on individual, collegial, and organizational improvement;

♦ Respects and nurtures the intellectual and leadership capacity of teachers, principals, and others in the school community;

♦ Reflects the best available research and practice in teaching, learning, and leadership;

♦ Enables teachers to develop further expertise in subject content, teaching strategies, uses of technologies, and other essential elements of teaching to high standards;

♦ Promotes continuous inquiry and improvement embedded in the daily life of schools;

♦ Is planned collaboratively by those who will participate in and facilitate that development;

♦ Requires substantial time and resources;

♦ Is driven by a coherent long-term plan;

♦ Is evaluated ultimately on the basis of its effects on teacher instruction and student learning, and uses this assessment to guide subsequent professional development efforts.

Source: U.S. Department of Education (1995). *Building Bridges: The Mission and Principles of Professional Development*. Retrieved October 13, 2002, from http://www.ed.gov/G2K/bridge.html.

Through collaboration, teachers are able to support growth and development while improving their practices. Collaboration includes such activities as co-planning and teaching lessons, brainstorming ideas, conducting action research, and inter-classroom observations (peer coaching), and the reflection and dialogue that follows in post-observation conferences. To break the prevalent patterns of teacher isolation, time and the commitment of the principal are needed. Collaborative cultures send strong messages to teachers and students about the seriousness of the work accomplished in the classroom. Students benefit in collaborative cultures when teachers work toward the betterment of instructional practices.

Trust

Trust is a prerequisite for building a positive school climate and culture. Without trust, efforts to build a healthy culture will be diminished. Without trust, relationships will flounder. Trust and respect build a strong foundation for the work and efforts of teachers. Bryk and Schneider (2002) identify "relational trust" as the core ingredient for school improvement. Relational trust rests on a foundation of respect, personal regard, and integrity. Relational trust flourishes when all members of the school are encouraged to contribute, learn, and be part of the discussion about teaching and student learning.

Building and maintaining trust evolves over time. Trust is built on its history in the organization and the history of trust between teachers and administrators. A leader must ask several questions:

+ Do teachers trust me?

+ Do teachers have confidence in my actions?

+ Do my words and actions align with each other?

+ Do teachers believe I hold them in high regard?

+ Do I exhibit integrity in the way I make decisions, communicate expectations, and allocate resources?

+ What behaviors have in the past eroded trust in the leadership of the school?

The answers to these questions can serve as a guide to self-discovery about the patterns of trust and the work needed to build more trusting relationships with teachers.

Pulling it All Together

The homepage for the Dassel-Cokato Middle School (DCMS) illustrates the *unity* of purpose in Principal Jeff Powers's message, the school's mission statement, and the objectives to meet the mission. However, Powers and his faculty went beyond these purposes. They developed the ideal attributes of teachers at DCMS, and how every program offered to students and their families of this school relate directly to the vision and mission of the school.

A Vision of Possibilities

Dassel-Cokato Middle School
Mr. Jeff Powers, Principal
P.O. Box 1500
4852 Reardon Ave. S.W.
Cokato, MN 55321
jpowers@admin.dc.k12.mn.us
Phone: (320) 286–4100 ext. 1600
Fax: (320) 286–4176
http://www.dc.k12.mn.us/MSCHOOL/Default.htm

The Principal's Welcome Message

Welcome to Our School.

Thank you for visiting the Dassel-Cokato Middle School (DCMS) website. My name is Jeff Powers and I have the pleasure of being the DCMS principal. Our commitment to continuous improvement, and strong partnerships with families, provides us with the foundation that we need as we strive to help every student succeed. As your children attend DCMS, or if you are contemplating sending your children here, I am confident that you will find that we have a very knowledgeable, dedicated staff and a safe, supportive environment. Please contact me with any questions, ideas, or to arrange a tour of our program. I look forward to hearing from you!

The Mission Statement

D-CMS Serving Students

The mission of the Dassel-Cokato Middle School is to encourage a positive attitude towards learning while preparing students with transferable and meaningful skills for life in a global society.

The Dassel-Cokato Middle School program is designed to meet the special needs of middle level students. The program strives to be transitional in nature, providing students the "bridge" between the self-contained classroom of the elementary school and the departmentalized curriculum of the high school.

Beliefs and Values of the Dassel-Cokato Middle School Teachers and Administrators

We Believe the Dassel-Cokato Middle School Should:

♦ Meet the unique needs of early adolescents.

♦ Be child centered.

♦ Reflect the values and priorities of the community, parents, and students.

♦ Provide students the opportunity to explore a wide variety of interests and skills.

♦ Offer many opportunities for students to be successful physically, socially, emotionally, and intellectually.

♦ Recognize and reward their successes.

♦ Encourage individual differences and attempt to meet unique student needs.

♦ Develop in students a respect for themselves and others.

♦ Develop in students a sense of interdependence and belonging.

♦ Emphasize academically challenging experiences that fosters thinking, problem solving and develop an attitude for life-long learning.

♦ Emphasize an allied arts curriculum that stimulates creativity, enjoyment, and knowledge.

Meeting the Goals of the Vision

To achieve the broad goals of this vision, the Dassel-Cokato Middle School recognizes the importance of the environment in which children work. If we expect them to develop individual capacities in a wide variety of activities, the setting must be flexible and allow for risk taking. Worthwhile social attitudes can only be expected where both the children and adults have respect for one another, are friendly, and care for each other's needs.

Dassel-Cokato Middle School—
Teacher Attributes

In order to reach the goals implied in the Dassel-Cokato Middle School Vision and to successfully implement the Characteristics of the Middle School, the middle school teacher should have:

- A willingness to conduct a teacher advisor group of students.

- A belief that it is better to recognize and reward positive student growth, than it is to focus undue attention on the negative.

- A willingness to share teaching methods and techniques with fellow colleagues in team planning process.

- A willingness to try different ways of presenting information for students.

- A willingness to cooperative learning, develop lessons appropriate for different learning style's, and use other appropriate methods that will help enhance students' chances for success.

- A willingness to become involved in teaching exploratory program for students.

- A willingness to involve the community and parents in the education of their children.

- A willingness to get involved in summer writing time as needed.

- A willingness to change and take risks.

- A belief those students are more important than the content.

Programs At Dassel-Cokato Middle School
that Reflect the Mission and Values of the School

Teacher Advisor Program: A program that will build student social skills, develop a sense of belonging, teach group skills, encourage self-respect and appreciation for others and provide instruction in study skills.

Academic Programs: Emphasis should remain on the acquisition of basic and more advanced skills even though more attention is given to developing the child socially, emotionally and physically. Assurance of mastery of basic skills, remediation of special needs, enrichment programs extending the basic curriculum and gifted program activities are all key components.

Allied Arts Programs: Early adolescents have individual strengths and talents that can be developed only through instruction in areas of art, music, physical education, home economics and industrial arts. Co-curricular and extra-curricular programs should emphasize broad student participation to enable each and every student a chance to participate in their area of interest.

Positive Recognition Philosophy: Realizing that no one does anything for nothing, that there must always be some payoff, it is better to recognize and reward positive student growth so that positive behavior and attitudes are fostered.

Interdisciplinary Team Planning: Team planning facilitates integrated studies as well as allows teacher the opportunity to develop specific programs for students with unique needs. It takes full advantage of teacher strengths and makes home and student communication more feasible.

Flexible Scheduling: The schedule must allow teachers and students the freedom to control the amount and kind of instruction required to ensure student success. It must permit teacher advisor time, interdisciplinary team planning, exploratory programs, the development of interdisciplinary units and time for implementing the positive recognition philosophy.

Community and Parent Involvement: Members of the community and the parents will ultimately decide the quality of our service, therefore, being responsive to the community and parents can not only help us reach our goals but can help us become accountable and ensure our success.

Student Support Groups: Providing for the social and emotional needs of students supports classroom instruction and makes student success more likely. Guidance that is flexible and personalized will enhance the other programs in the school.

Interdisciplinary Units: Interdisciplinary education, encompassing academics and allied arts, will increase students' understanding go the world they live in and fore them to use higher level thinking skills., These units will also foster reference and locational skills as well as promoting the use of visual aids, media center resources and other skills needed for continued lifelong learning.

Student Organizations: Clubs and organization offer students the opportunity to explore, expand and develop new interests while providing application of social and group skills. These activities develop a sense of belonging and bring a positive attitude about school.

Teacher Support Groups: Teachers must be actively involved with their colleagues in planning instruction and in developing improved teaching methods. While empowering the staff, there must also be training and support programs that permit individual staff growth and personal development.

Orientation Program: Programs to help students and parents function in a new situation are critical to the success of the middle school. These programs should offer a time for developing student-teacher-parent relationships, conveying information about program offerings and sharing the school and classroom vision.

Parent Education Programs: Because parents play such an important role in their children's social, emotional, intellectual and physical attitudes it is necessary to actively involve parents in their children's' education. It may also be necessary to train the parents to be more effective in their role of teacher and provide support for them as they attempt to deal with their early adolescent.

Suggested Reading

Barth, R. S. (2001). *Learning by heart.* San Francisco, CA: Jossey-Bass.

Fielder, D. J. (2003). *Achievement now! How to assure no child is left behind.* Larchmont, NY: Eye on Education.

Hammonds, B. (2002). Quality learning. At leading-learning.co.nz. Retrieved November 16, 2002, from http://www.leading-learning.co.nz/school- vision/vision-process.html.

Kouzes, J. M., & Posner, B. Z. (2001). *The leadership challenge: How to keep getting extraordinary things done in organizations* (3rd ed.. San Francisco, CA: Jossey-Bass.

Schlechty, P. C. (1997). *Inventing better schools: An action plan for educational reform.* San Francisco, CA: Jossey-Bass.

Short, R., & Greer, J. (1997). *Leadership for empowered schools.* Columbus, OH: Merrill.

Speck, M. (1999). *The principalship: Building a learning community.* Upper Saddle River, NJ: Prentice Hall.

3

Supervision, Staff Development, and Teacher Evaluation

Instructional Leaders Connect Supervision, Staff Development, and Teacher Evaluation as Seamless Practices

In this Chapter . . .

♦ Connecting the dots—supervision, staff development, and teacher evaluation

♦ Focus on the adult learner

♦ Planning for staff development

♦ Job-embedded staff development

♦ An overview of staff development models that link to instructional supervision

For both students and teachers, learning does not occur in a black box as a series of discrete activities. McQuarrie and Wood (1991) believe that "supervision [and] staff development is more than distinct, independent processes that can be employed to improve instruction. They should be considered part of a comprehensive approach to improve instructional practices" (p. 94). Teachers, as the instructional leaders of their classrooms, design instruction that fits the learning needs of their students. As the instructional leader, the principal is the "teacher of teachers." In this capacity, it is the duty of the principal to provide a program in which instructional supervision, staff development, teacher evaluation, and any other activities (e.g., peer coaching and mentoring) are unified in purpose and intent—teacher growth and development to ensure that students get the absolutely best from their teachers.

Supervision, staff development, and evaluation are the basic building blocks that effective schools use to construct the foundation of a learning organization. Therefore, if consistent growth is to occur on an individual or organizational basis, then time and effort must be appropriated for the work involved in connecting the dots between and among supervision, staff development, evaluation.

Connecting the Dots—Supervision, Staff Development, and Teacher Evaluation

Supervision Is Not a Linear, Lockstep Process

Instructional supervision, clinical supervision, or any other form of in-classroom supervision (peer coaching) that aims to foster the professional growth of teachers cannot be reduced to a lockstep, linear process with a fixed beginning or end. The processes involved in supervision, staff development, teacher evaluation, and the like must be cyclical and ongoing. The process known as *clinical supervision* was originally designed to continue in cycles, with each cycle (pre-observation, observation, and post-observation) informing future cycles and identifying the activities needed to help teachers meet their learning objectives.

Staff development and teacher evaluation must be linked to supervision, perhaps even embedded within and throughout each cycle of supervision. What is needed is a model that connects the various forms of assistance available to teachers. However, no one model can ever be expected to fit the needs of every teacher and the contexts in which they work. There are ways to bring together supervision, staff development, evaluation, and other activities such as peer coaching and mentoring. The real charge for principals is to unify these efforts. One way to start is to scan your own school building to determine what support systems in addition to clinical supervision are in place for teachers. Figure 3.1 is an example of how to track these programs.

Teachers are the central actors in the learning process. In the final analysis, they are the ones who *control* internally what is (or is not) learned through schoolwide efforts such as peer coaching or portfolio development, as well as in the traditional clinical model of supervision.

Figure 3.1. Examining Teacher Support Programs

Identify the professional development and supervisory opportunities available in your school building. In the first column, list these opportunities. In the second column, describe how the opportunities link to one another.

Professional Development and Supervisory Opportunities	*How These Opportunities are Linked*
Peer Coaching	Numerous peer coaches serve as mentors, coaching teachers through direct classroom observation that includes both pre- and post-observation conferences.
Mentoring and Induction	The induction program includes mentoring, peer coaching, and study groups.
Study Groups	Teachers form study groups and examine instructional issues; groups may read common materials; some teachers are involved in peer coaching; some teachers extend study group activities with teacher-directed action research.
Portfolio Development	Action research teams are developing portfolios to track changes in practice.
Action Research Teams	Groups of teachers conduct action research on classroom practices and stay with a problem of practice for an extended period.

Linking Instructional Supervision, Staff Development, and Teacher Evaluation

In *The Centerless Corporation: A New Model for Transforming Your Organization for Growth and Prosperity,* Pasternack and Viscio (1998) describe a type of unity they call coherence.

> Coherence is what holds the firm together. It is the glue that binds the various pieces, enabling them to act as one. It includes a broad range of processes. It begins with a shared vision and shared set of values, and expands to include numerous linkages across the company. (p. 61)

This shared vision and set of values link supervision, staff development, evaluation, and other learning opportunities, but more importantly, relates and unifies them. Woven together in a holistic way, learning opportunities follow their own course while contributing to the overall development of the faculty and the school.

To be valuable, an approach must be flexible, adaptable to a particular environment, and shaped by the people who apply it. Figure 3.2 presents one approach to linking supervision, staff development, evaluation, and other forms of development (such as peer coaching, action research, and portfolio development) in a way that fosters coherence.

This approach offers a framework for unifying professional development and supervisory initiatives. Implicit assumptions are that the work of the principal is recursive and that all approaches to supervision, staff development, and evaluation employ processes that promote growth, including reflection, inquiry, and dialogue. The basic premise is that supervision, staff development, and teacher evaluation form a seamless web. This web is formative and cyclical, and Figure 3.3 (p. 62) illustrates the formative and cyclical nature of supervision, staff development, and teacher evaluation.

This approach offers a framework for unifying professional development and supervisory initiatives. Implicit assumptions are that the work of the principal is recursive and that all approaches to supervision, staff development, and evaluation employ processes that promote growth, including reflection, inquiry, and dialogue. The basic premise is that supervision, staff development, and teacher evaluation form a seamless web. This web is formative and cyclical, and Figure 3.3 (p. 62) illustrates the formative and cyclical nature of supervision, staff development, and teacher evaluation.

Given the magnitude of the formative nature of supervision, staff development, and teacher evaluation, the remainder of this chapter is devoted to staff development, squarely centered in the middle of Figure 3.3. This break occurs

(Text continues on page 62.)

Figure 3.2. Unifying Instructional Supervision, Staff Development, and Teacher Evaluation

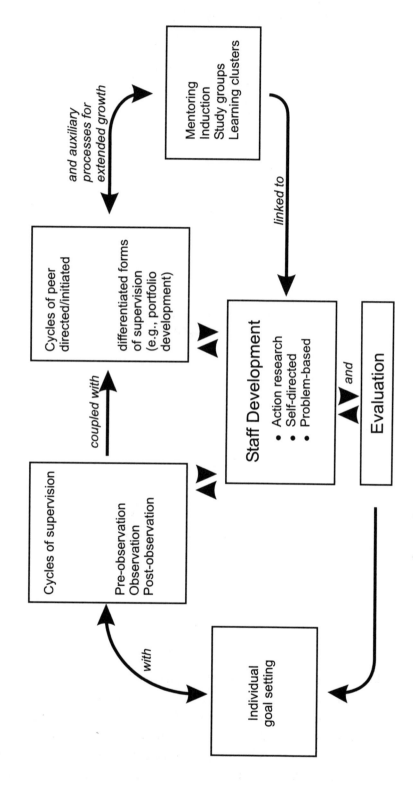

Figure 3.3. The Formative Nature of Supervision, Staff Development, and Teacher Evaluation

because staff development is a tool for the principal. Staff development is often a follow-up to a classroom observation; however, supervision is often a follow-up to staff development. Silently embedded across all efforts and as a precursor to success in supervision, staff development, and teacher evaluation are the adult learning needs of teachers. Supervision, staff development, and teacher evaluation have one primary common denominator—the teacher as an adult learner.

Focus on the Adult Learner

School districts across the United States spend over 80 percent of their budgets on staff salaries. Given this expenditure, opportunities for professional development need to be elevated as a top priority if schools are to realize maximum return on this investment. With new federal legislation raising the accountability bar to new heights, the business of supporting the professional development needs of teachers can no longer remain on the proverbial "to do list" of busy school administrators. Just like the students that teachers teach, adults have learning needs that must be met or efforts toward providing staff development, supervision, and teacher evaluation as a seamless process will be wasted.

There are many perspectives on adult learning. There are patterns that have been teased from the research and the professional literature that can assist the principal in framing learning opportunities—primarily through supervision, staff development, and teacher evaluation—the processes that principals can direct to more positive ends. Figure 3.4 offers perspectives about learning opportunities for adults from the National Commission on Teaching and America's Future (1996) and the National Foundation for Improving Education (1996). The reader is encouraged to examine the Standards for Staff Development (National Staff Development Council) in their entirety at http://www.mdk12.org/ instruction/leadership/staff_development/nsdc.html.

Both of these reports call for fundamental change in the ways in which teachers work with one another and, by implication, the very ways in which principals work with teachers. Just like the effective teacher, the effective principal understands the needs of learners, and, in the case of the principal, teachers as learners. A principal can understand the learning needs of teachers in several ways. One such way is to understand career stages.

Career Stage Theories and the Career Stage Continuum

Principals help teachers become fully functioning professionals by recognizing their developmental needs and affording learning opportunities that meet those needs. A first step is to assess teachers' needs by examining career stages and the generalized principles that characterize adult learning within a particular stage.

Fuller (1969) very broadly identifies three stages of teacher's concerns: preteaching phase = nonconcern; early teaching phase = concern with self; and late teaching phase = concern with pupils. Figure 3.5 (p. 65) highlights Fuller's stages of concern.

(Text continues on page 65.)

Figure 3.4. National Perspectives on Learning Opportunities for Adults

The National Commission on Teaching and America's Future recommends that learning be

- connected to teacher's work with their students;
- linked to concrete tasks of teaching;
- organized around problem solving;
- informed by research; and
- sustained over time by ongoing conversations and coaching.

Source: National Commission on Teaching and America's Future, 1996, p. 43.

The National Foundation for Improving Education believes schools need to promote activities that

- have the goal of improving student learning at the heart of every school endeavor;
- help teachers and other school staff meet future needs of students who learn in different ways and who come from diverse cultural, linguistic, and socioeconomic backgrounds;
- provide adequate time for inquiry, reflection, and mentoring and is an important part of the normal working day of all public educators;
- are rigorous, sustained, and adequate to the long-term change of practice;
- are directed toward teachers' intellectual development and leadership;
- foster a deepening of subject-matter knowledge, a greater understanding of learning, and a greater appreciation of students' needs;
- are designed and directed by teachers, incorporates the best principles of adult learning, and involve shared decisions designed to improve the school;
- balance individual priorities with school and district needs and advance the profession as a whole;
- make best use of new technologies; [and],
- are site based and supportive of a clearly articulated vision for students.

Source: National Foundation for Improving Education, 1996, pp. 6–7.

Figure 3.5. Fuller's Stages of Concern

Stage of Concern	*Motivation*	*Description*
Survival	External	Seeks approval and affirmation from peers and administrators. Time spent primarily on coping with the immediacy of complex and unfamiliar situations and making decisions.
Task Stage	External	Focuses on tasks that need to be implemented.
Impact Stage	Internal	Focuses on meeting the needs of learners; self-growth and development are attended to through learning new skills and refining existing practices based on cues from students.

Source: Fuller, 1969.

Huberman (1993), relying on concepts of developmental psychology, indicates that teachers travel through several stages:

- ◆ survival and discovery (feelings of fear and enthusiasm);
- ◆ stabilization;
- ◆ emancipation and diversification (or possible stagnation);
- ◆ reassessment;
- ◆ serenity and relational distance;
- ◆ conservatism and complaints; and
- ◆ disengagement.

Huberman (1993) cautions that not all teachers move through all these stages, that movement is unpredictable, and that not all teachers move through these stages at the same rate or intensity. Figure 3.6 depicts dominant ideas about teacher stage and career development. Principals are encouraged to think about their teachers while reviewing this table. The exercise might yield insight on providing growth opportunities (supervision, staff development, evaluation) that match the needs of teachers.

Figure 3.6. Career Stages and Developmental Needs

Stage	Name	Years in Field (approximate)	Developmental Theory and Needs
1	Pre-service	0	Training and preparation for a profession.
2	Induction	1–2	Survival stage (Burden, 1982; Feiman & Floden, 1980): Seeks safety and desires to learn the day-to-day operations of the school and the complexities of facing new situations in the classroom.
3	Competency	3–5	Confidence in work mounts as does understanding. Building of the multifaceted role of teaching.
4	Enthusiasm	5–8	Actively seeks out professional development and other opportunities for professional growth; high job satisfaction (Burke, Christensen, & Fessler, 1984, p. 15).
5	Career frustration	Varies	Teacher burnout (Burke, Christensen, & Fessler, 1984, p. 15).
6	Stability	Varies	Complacency sets in; innovation is low.
7	Career wind-down	Varies	Coasts through on past laurels; status lets the teacher get by without exerting much effort.
8	Career exit	Varies	End of a teaching career.

Source: Adapted from Burden (1982); Burke, Christensen, & Fessler (1984); Christensen, Burke, Fessler, & Hagstrom (1983); Feiman & Floden (1980); Huberman, 1993; Katz, 1972; Newman, Dornburg, Dubois, & Kranz (1980).

One caveat: Identifying the stages of teacher development is tricky business, because there are no absolutes. A teacher's practice, beliefs, and knowledge will change through experiences gained on the job, formal coursework taken in graduate schools, participation in site and district-wide staff development opportunities, and personal lifetime events. Burden's (1982) research indicates that teacher experience changes occur over time in

- ♦ job skills, knowledge, and behaviors—in areas such as teaching methods, discipline strategies, and curriculum planning;

- ♦ attitudes and outlooks—in areas such as images of teaching, professional confidence and maturity, willingness to try new teaching methods, and concerns; and

- ♦ job events—in areas such as changes in grade level, school, or district; involvement in additional professional responsibilities; and age of entry and retirement. (pp. 1–2)

Newman, Burden, and Applegate (1980) developed a method to take the guesswork out of this process—*ask teachers themselves to identify where they are.* They suggest that principals have teachers identify their own current stage of development and its markers. Figure 3.7 highlights this process more fully. After introducing the idea at a faculty meeting, the principal could meet with each teacher individually to discuss markers and needs for meeting goals.

Figure 3.7. Assessing Teacher Career Stages

Process

1. Have teachers draw a horizontal line across the blank page. This represents the time line of their teaching careers.

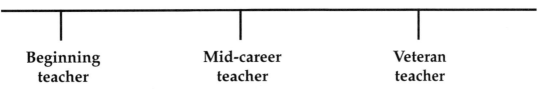

| Beginning teacher | Mid-career teacher | Veteran teacher |

2. Say, "Careers may be marked by different stages, experiences, changes. If you were to divide your teaching career into several parts, what would mark your divisions? Mark them down on the line. Jot down the special characteristics of each part" (p. 8).

3. After teachers have identified where they are in their careers, the supervisor needs to provide a forum for sharing this "private" information.

Source: Newman, Burden, & Applegate, 1980

Identifying the characteristics of a school's faculty is not simple. The process of thinking about adult learning starts with getting to know your people as adult learners, eager to refine the practices that shape their classroom practices.

Know Your People

The following activity (Figure 3.8) can assist in *broadly* profiling a school's faculty by gathering statistical information about its members. A faculty sign-in sheet offers a tool to help track and tally information.

Figure 3.8. Assessing the Characteristics of a Faculty

1. Number of teachers _____ Male _____ Female _____

2. For each teacher, indicate the number of years in teaching and then total the number of years of experience. _____

   Then, calculate the average years of faculty experience. _____

3. Number of teachers whose experience falls years in the ranges:

   a. 1 to 3 years _____ b. 4 to 7 years _____ c. 8 to 11 years _____

   d. 12 to 15 years _____ e. 16 to 19 years _____ f. 20+ years _____

4. Number of first-year teachers _____

5. Number of teachers who will retire at the end of the year _____

6. Wild cards:

   First-year teachers with experience _____

   Alternatively certified teachers _____

   Teachers returning to work after an extended leave _____

   Other _____

7. What overall patterns do you notice?

The patterns a principal discovers about a faculty can provide a basis for understanding the overall learning needs of teachers. The information gleaned from such a profile is very broad; in a sense, it relates to all but to none. The principal needs to dig deeper to uncover more about *each* teacher. Expanding on the information collected in Figure 3.8 yields a profile of the faculty (or a group of teachers, such as a department or a grade level). Figure 3.9 gives an example of information that describes the general characteristics of *specific* teachers.

Figure 3.9. Faculty Profile

Teacher	Years of Experience	Highest Degree	Specialized Training
Baker	7	B.S.	Cooperative learning applied to math.
Davis	15	M.A. + 15 Spanish & French	Spent 3 months in Spain.
Franklin	2 (15 years prior experience as a chemist)	Ph.D. (alternatively certified) Chemistry	Unknown

Planning for Staff Development

In public schools, staff development often consists of a series of isolated events called workshops that teachers attend outside of the workday. Hirsh and Ponder (1991) conclude that on the strength of a workshop alone, only about 10 percent of teachers are able to transfer newly learned skills into daily practice, and according to McBride, Reed, and Dollar (1994), only 12.6 percent of teachers reported any meaningful follow-up to determine if skills learned in staff development workshops were being implemented in the classroom. Principals are in an advantageous position to identify staff development needs and to provide the follow-up support teachers need to implement new skills into their daily practices.

Staff development is effective when it meet goals and aligns to the needs of site personnel and the organization. The principal can begin thinking about staff development by asking five general questions:

1. What staff development is needed?

2. What planning for staff development needs to be completed?

3. What resources are needed to provide staff development?

4. What follow-up activities are needed to support the application and extension of skills learned in staff development?

5. How can the overall impact of staff development on student and teacher learning be evaluated?

The answer to these questions can serve as a guide for framing staff development. The principal (especially a new one to a system) should do some up-front work to find out the history of staff development in the school and the district. Consulting with the district staff development contact person will help to acquaint the principal with the district's vision of staff development. Examining artifacts such as descriptions of staff development offerings will help the principal discover when staff development is offered (during the year, summer), who offers staff development (outside consultants, district-wide personnel), and where staff development is conducted (at site buildings, district central office, college/university campus).

At the site level, the principal needs to uncover:

♦ Who conducts staff development?

♦ Who decides what staff development should be made available?

♦ Does staff development align with site-level goals?

♦ Are there processes in place for teachers to request staff development?

The answers to these questions will help the principal understand the history of staff development at both the site and district levels and gain insight on how and if staff development between these two levels align.

Identifying Staff Development Needs

Methods of identifying staff development needs include *informal discussion* (e.g., during planning periods, over lunch), *formal discussions* (e.g., faculty meetings, department, team, or grade-level meetings), *faculty surveys*, and *classroom observations*. A tracking sheet offered in Figure 3.10 can assist the principal in (1) tracking identified staff development needs, (2) making connections between identified needs, and (3) identifying strategies to meet those needs.

Perhaps nothing is more hurried than the schedule of a K–12 teacher. Therefore, making every minute count becomes a necessity, and principals need to learn how to scan the environment, looking for opportunities for teachers to learn. However, before developing learning opportunities for adults, principals need to know *what needs to be learned and by whom*. Opportunities abound for principals to talk with teachers and include time during planning periods and lunch periods to engage teachers in discussion about teaching. In the relaxed atmosphere of the faculty lunchroom, teachers tend to be more comfortable participating in candid discussions about teaching. During informal discussions, the principal can work as a prospector, searching for hidden "nuggets" that can be further examined through more formal discussions in a department, grade-level, or team meeting or become a focus in future classroom observations.

The principal can purposefully link supervision and staff development through classroom observations. Needs can also be identified through more

Figure 3.10. Tracking Staff Development Needs

Need	Teacher(s) Requesting/Needing	In-House Resources	Strategy
Cooperative Learning	Temple, Vanderhoof, Witt	Ms. Patton	Two workshops, model teaching unit by Ms. Patton, and then extension via classroom observations
Classroom Management	All-district mandated	Assistant Principal Smith	Workshop on district classroom management policy; individual meetings with each grade-level/ team/department member; classroom observations; follow-up meetings
Integrating Technology	Denton, Watson, Younger	Dr. Vardaman (Computer Science Teacher)	Workshop, model teaching unit by Dr. Vardaman; follow-up meetings with each teacher

formal means such as informal and formal classroom observations, and this is the value of making classroom observations a priority. Through analysis of data collected and the discussion that occurs during the pre-and post-observation conferences, the principal can help teachers identify techniques that can help enhance strategies already in use in the classroom, as well as new strategies or potential problem areas that need attention.

Since much of the planning for staff development occurs before each school year begins, some schools distribute surveys so that teachers can formally indicate what they want and need to learn. Ideally, there is alignment between site-level goals and the staff development offered at the site. Figure 3.11 (p. 72) offers a sample questionnaire.

Once identified, appropriate staff development for supporting needs can be developed with the principal and teacher leaders helping fellow teachers achieve identified goals through the staff development offered at the site level.

Figure 3.11. Staff Development Questionnaire

App Middle School

Name: _____ Date: _____

1. Considering our school goals in the areas of assessment, technological applications, and integrated learning, are there specific areas within these goals that you would like to explore next year and for which you feel you would benefit from involvement in staff development activities?

2. What kinds of activities (workshops, collaborative meetings, planning time, in-the-classroom support, formal coursework, etc.) do you feel would most benefit you in your support of the school goals?

3. Are there other areas in which you are interested—classroom management, specific projects, curriculum materials, idea exchanges, discussion groups, etc.?

4. Are there areas in which you have been working that you have developed proficiency to be a leader and resource for other teachers in the school or district?

Teacher Expertise—A Rich Resource for Learning

As staff development needs are identified, strategies to meet those needs should be taking form. Often, district and site staff developers look immediately to outside facilitators to support their staff development programs. In the process, myriad resources within the district or site are overlooked. At the beginning of the school year, principals are encouraged to "solicit" volunteers to assist with in-house staff development. Think of the potential in any given school. For the most part, teachers are lifelong learners, and they continually attend workshops, graduate school courses, and other specialized training opportunities to add to their repertoire of skills.

Teachers attend to their own learning during the school year and during the summer, and they often pay entirely or partially for these learning opportunities. Teachers return to the schoolhouse with new knowledge and new skills, eager to them implement in their classrooms. However, follow-up support and encouragement from those who plan staff development is often missing.

One of the ironies in the work lives of teachers is that they often do not have the opportunity to share with others what they have learned. Effective principals find opportunities for teachers to share their expertise with others. The first step in the process is to identify expertise among teachers, and this can be achieved by *asking* teachers to self-identify their expertise and willingness to share knowledge with others. Two strategies include:

1. Developing a self-reporting survey distributed at the beginning of the school year (Figure 3.12, p. 74)

2. Tracking staff development and training that teacher's attend throughout the year (Figure 3.13, p. 74)

A second way to track teacher expertise is to keep a record of what staff development teachers attend throughout the school year and summer. Often, school systems pay teachers to attend staff development during the year and summer, and teachers need to request funds and substitute teachers to attend workshops and seminars. In addition to the principal, others such as lead teachers, instructional coordinators, and department chairs could easily develop a database to keep track of this information.

Using Faculty Meetings for Staff Development

Most schools hold faculty meetings—some weekly, biweekly, or monthly. Regardless of the faculty-meeting configuration, faculty meetings provide opportunities for staff development opportunities and the promotion of staff collaboration. Much of the information that is shared during faculty meetings can easily be distributed by memo, e-mail, or in a faculty bulletin. Principals are encouraged to work with their teachers to design and implement strategies for using faculty meeting time for providing learning opportunities for teachers.

The faculty meeting can become a powerful forum for staff development when teachers who attend workshops and seminars paid for by the school system present what was learned. The following suggestions can assist the principal in framing the faculty meeting as a learning opportunity.

♦ Introduce the teacher and the name of the conference or seminar the teacher attended.

♦ Publicize the topic and presenters in the weekly memo, send an all-school e-mail, or use the meeting agenda.

Figure 3.12. Faculty Expertise Survey

Dear Colleagues:

Every year we update our Teacher Expertise Pool. Please take a few minutes to review the following areas and check those in which you have expertise and are willing to share your knowledge with others. Looking forward to hearing from you,

Paula

1. Peer Coaching _____
2. Phonics _____
3. Literacy _____
4. Math Our Way Series _____
5. Writing across the Curriculum _____
6. Big Book lesson planning _____
7. Authentic Assessment and Rubrics _____
8. Technology Applications _____

9. Portfolio Development _____
10. At-Risk Children _____
11. Reluctant Learners _____
12. Outdoor Education _____
13. Science Fair _____
14. Music and Art Therapy _____
15. Conflict Resolution _____
16. Other: _____

Name:_____ (optional)

Figure 3.13. Database: Teacher Professional Development

Teacher	Conference or Workshop	Dates	Date follow-up presentation made to the faculty (meeting date)	Resources needed for follow-up
Arnold	Cooperative Learning for Special Needs Students	10/23/01	11/09/01	Preview video series on cooperative learning; purchase workbooks for teachers; possible full day in-service for staff—check with central office for funding.
Asher	Managing Aggression in Students	3/24–27/02	4/11/02; 4/14/02 (PTA presentation)	Schedule a meeting with counselors and social workers in the school cluster; books recommended by Asher.

◆ Allow sufficient time by asking the teacher to project how much time is needed.

◆ Include time for teachers to ask questions, discuss implications, or work in small groups.

◆ Videotape the presentation and keep a copy of the tape in the library. By the end of the year, there should be a sizeable collection of learning materials. These materials will be helpful for newcomers to the staff in subsequent years.

◆ Assist teachers with developing a handout about the content of the seminar (or be ready to provide secretarial support to reproduce materials from the seminar) before the faculty meeting.

◆ Follow up after the faculty meeting with a summary of the discussion. Seek additional learning materials for faculty based on needs or interest generated during the faculty meeting. Consult with district staff to obtain additional resources.

Forming a Staff Development Planning Team

One way to transform faculty meetings into learning opportunities is to develop a planning committee that would help to shape the focus of faculty meetings throughout the year. The staff development planning committee could meet a few weeks before the school year begins to plan. The committee could include the lead teacher, the instructional coordinator, or one or two grade-level leaders or department chairs in addition to either the principal or the assistant principal. Much of the configuration of the committee will depend on the level—elementary, middle, or high school.

The names of the individuals on the planning committee could be published in a staff bulletin or memo, so that all the teachers can give their ideas to one of the individuals on the staff development planning committee. The key is to get teachers talking about their professional development needs.

After staff development needs have been identified, a yearlong agenda with a time line based on the consensus of the teachers' staff development needs can be developed. Once the agenda of topics is identified, leadership among the members of the staff development committee can be shared—lining up teachers to present or conduct the staff development, with the principal or a teacher (or both) acting as facilitator, timekeeper, or recorder during faculty meetings or in-service days. The agenda and focus of the staff development can be varied. For instance, some topics may deal with faculty interests, while others may relate more to district initiatives or school goals. Sometimes, simply sharing a specific teaching technique makes for a stimulating staff development topic. Figure 3.14 offers a summary form of in-house staff development human resources.

Figure 3.14. In-House Staff Development Human Resources

Teacher	Subject(s) Taught	Areas of Expertise/Interest
Allison	Mathematics	Integrating Technology in Instruction
Clay	Mathematics	Classroom Management
Jay	Science	Modifying Instruction for Diverse Learners
Patton	Social Studies	Cooperative Learning; Socratic Seminars
Rascoe	English	Calling Patterns as a Classroom Management Tool

This form will expand as expertise and willingness to share expertise grows. In addition to potential workshop facilitators, the process of identifying "in-house" staff development expertise might also assist principals to locate faculty members with expertise and interest in various staff development and supervision models such as peer coaching, action research, reflection, and portfolio development. Other sources of staff development support include regional service centers, area universities, and state departments of education.

Identifying staff developers inside and outside of the district or site is just the first step in planning for staff development. Because workshops alone do not adequately support teacher growth, a comprehensive plan that promotes continuous learning is needed. Although no magic formula for planning and conducting staff development exists, some general strategies that help to promote ongoing learning include establishing the initiative, developing a follow-up plan, and creating a method for assessing the initiative.

Readying for Staff Development

For staff development to be successful, participants need to understand the purpose of the initiative, how the initiative is to be carried out, what is expected of each participant in the initiative, as well as a voice in selecting and planning the initiative. These "housekeeping tasks" also help *to ready* teachers for staff development and to reinforce the message that the initiative is important. Figure 3.15 offers a plan for the principal to ensure that teachers are ready for staff development.

The most common way of accomplishing these tasks is to hold an introductory meeting. Introductory meetings have three basic purposes: (1) to ready participants for the initiative, (2) to make decisions about how the initiative will

Figure 3.15. Staff Readiness Planning Matrix

Purpose of the initiative	How the initiative is to be carried out	What is expected of each participant in the initiative	Planning the initiative
Increase student attendance and decrease number of students arriving late to school.	Familiarize teachers with the problem. Brainstorm sessions at each grade level; review suggestions and ideas from each grade level.	Participate in framing the problem and in grade-level meetings.	Distribute a survey for input on staff development needed to work with students and families. Seek volunteers from the faculty to attend a weeklong workshop and commit to providing staff development for the staff.

be carried out, and (3) to disperse needed information. The principal will learn much from the introductory meeting, namely, which direction in planning is necessary to launch a schoolwide staff development plan.

Planning for Staff Development— Pulling the Pieces Together

There are numerous processes and steps to be taken in the planning for staff development, and the scope of this book does not allow for full coverage of each process. Figure 3.16 (p. 78) offers planning considerations for staff development.

By working through these questions and processes with others (such as a planning committee discussed earlier), the principal will be in a solid position to plan and to deliver staff development that is responsive to the needs of the teachers at the site.

Developing a Follow-up Plan and Assessing Staff Development

Because learning is a continuous process rather than a discrete event, support for learning must have a follow-up plan. The follow-up plan has two major purposes: (1) to monitor progress and (2) to provide feedback to participants. Monitoring is the process of ensuring that teachers have the support they need

Figure 3.16. Planning Considerations for Staff Development

1. Identify the objectives and goals of the plan.

2. Identify the target population (e.g., first-year teachers, fifth-grade math teachers, high school English teachers).

3. What are the needs of the teachers and staff who will be the benefactors of the staff development?

4. How were needs determined?

5. Who will be involved in the planning of the program?

6. How will these people be involved in planning?

7. What resources are needed? What are the costs of thee resources?

8. Detail the workings of the plan: What will be involved? What will teachers be doing (hopefully, more than just listening to someone)? What activities are planned for teachers? Identify the types of learning activities that will be embedded in the day-to-day work of teachers and how these activities will be embedded.

9. What types of ongoing support will be provided for teachers? How will this support be given and by whom?

10. How will you monitor the plan?

(release time, videotapes, access to professional journals) for learning. The intent of monitoring should never be confused with spying on teachers. An important facet of facilitating teacher learning is the process of providing feedback so that modifications, if needed, can be made. A simple check sheet similar to Figure 3.17 can be helpful in tracking follow-up efforts in staff development.

As important as planning is having a plan to assess the value and impact of the staff development. Resources in K–12 schools are too scarce to be wasted on staff development that does not help teachers to grow and students to learn. Moreover, since teachers' learning needs change over time, it is important to assess staff development to ensure its responsiveness to changes. There are two types of assessment: informal assessment and formal assessment. Both informal and formal assessments occurs across several levels—the assessment of the staff development, the assessment of how teachers are implementing staff development, and the assessment of the impact of staff development on student performance. Essentially, the principal wants to determine how teachers are using new knowledge and how staff development has benefited or enhanced student learning.

Figure 3.17. Staff Development Monitoring Form

Date	Teacher	Inquiry	Need Identified	Response
10/1	Mr. Bailey	What did you think of Ms. Denning's way of facilitating cooperative learning?	Mr. Bailey has not found time to observe Ms. Denning's class.	Locate a teacher to cover Mr. Bailey's class during one class period or teach Mr. Bailey's class.
10/2	Mr. Johnson	How is the videotape analysis coming?	Mr. Johnson needs additional videotapes; Mr. Porter, Johnson's partner, became ill.	Obtain additional videotapes and check to see how long Mr. Porter expects to be out and decide if Mr. Johnson should be assisted in securing a new partner for the time being.

Informal Assessment of Staff Development

Informal assessment occurs naturally during the follow-up process. All staff development meetings can end with a brief assessment. This can be a two- or three-question form soliciting feedback on the topics covered, the value of the discussion, and how staff might want to go further in learning more about a specific topic. Another way to assess the staff development meeting is by going around the room and asking each teacher to say one thing about the meeting that was personally valuable and indicate one area that could be improved. Incorporating feedback into future meetings will more than likely result in improved, more stimulating, and valuable staff participation and collaboration. Trust is a factor to consider.

Staff development is informally assessed while teachers are implementing new practices. The principal can use informal classroom observations and discussions in the hallway and faculty lounge as a means to assess how the content of staff development is being implemented. If there is a peer coaching or mentoring program at the site, peer coaches and mentors can help the principal assess what is occurring in classrooms because of staff development. The principal can seek to discover

- Skills teachers are implementing in practice
- Skills that teachers are struggling to implement
- What is working in practice—how and why
- The ongoing support and resources that teachers need
- Follow-up activities needed to support implementation
- Teachers who are willing to let others observe their teaching

The information from informal assessment can inform the ongoing direction of staff development for the remainder of the year and serve to confirm the findings of formal assessment.

Formal Assessment of Staff Development

Staff development needs to be evaluated formally through data collection and analysis. Commonly used data collection tools include survey instruments and focused interviews with participants. Survey instruments may consist of items that produce quantitative data, qualitative data, or both. Quantitative data are usually produced using a Likert scale (e.g., rating an item on a scale of 1 to 5), whereas qualitative data come from narrative responses to more open-ended questions (e.g., How did this workshop help you become a better teacher?).

Following collection, data need to be analyzed to identify patterns in the responses of either quantitative or qualitative assessments. These patterns can assist principals to identify strengths and weakness in staff development by looking at the intents of staff development—did the intents of the content of the staff development align with the needs? Moreover, data analysis can help principals to determine to what extent teachers have implemented a newly learned skill. The question to ask is, did implementation occur?

If staff development is linked to site goals and objectives (perhaps in the school improvement plan), data from formal sources such as standardized tests can be used to gauge what areas students are having difficulties in. These data can assist in identifying gaps in teacher knowledge or application of knowledge, and then staff development that will assist filling the gaps can be explored.

Job-Embedded Staff Development

Wood and Killian (1998) define *job-embedded learning* as "learning that occurs as teachers and administrators engage in their daily work activities" (p. 52). Sparks and Hirsh (1997) write that

Job-embedded learning ... links learning to the immediate and real-life problems faced by teachers and administrators. It is based on the assumption that the most powerful learning is that which occurs in response to challenges currently being faced by the learner and that allows for immediate application, experimentation, and adaptation on the job. (p. 52)

Job-embedded learning means that staff development is a continuous thread that can be found throughout the culture of a school. There are three attributes of successful job-embedded learning: (1) it is relevant to the individual teacher, (2) feedback is built into the process, and (3) it facilitates the transfer of new skills into practice.

First, because job-embedded learning is a part of the teacher's daily work, it is by its very nature relevant to the learner. Job-embedded learning addresses professional development goals and concerns of the individual teacher. In addition, job-embedded learning occurs *at the teacher's job site.* Therefore, the teacher's learning becomes an integral part of the culture of his/her classroom and school.

Second, through job-embedded learning, feedback is built in. Processes that can generate feedback include mentoring, peer coaching, reflection and dialogue, study groups, videotape analysis, and journaling. Teachers can use these tools to chronicle implementation of new instructional skills, provide artifacts for assessing transition from one learning activity to the next, or use as material to frame future initiatives.

Third, job-embedded staff development facilitates the transfer of new skills into practice. When ongoing support through the tools of job-embedded staff development is linked with instructional supervision, transfer of *skills into practice* becomes *part of the job.*

There are four essential conditions to ensure successful implementation of job-embedded staff development:

1. *Learning needs to be consistent with the principles of adult learning.* Learning goals are realistic, learning is relevant to the teacher, and concrete opportunities for practice of skills being learned are afforded.

2. *Trust in the process, in colleagues, and in the learner him/herself.* For learning to occur on the job, teachers must be able to trust the process (e.g., peer coaching, videotape analysis), their colleagues, and themselves. Teachers need to know that feedback will be constructive, not personal.

3. *Time within the regular school day needs to be made available for learning.* Traditionally, staff development takes place after hours, usually at some remote site. Job-embedded learning requires time to be avail-

able within the context of the normal working day at the teacher's school site.

4. *Sufficient resources must be available to support learning.* Providing release time for teachers' professional development requires the creative use of human resources. In addition, outside facilitators are sometimes needed to assist teachers in learning new skills. Funding must be made available to meet these costs. (Zepeda, 1999)

Benefits of quality job-embedded staff development are as varied as they are numerous. First, job-embedded learning can promote collegiality and trust among faculty members. Second, job-embedded learning empowers teachers since the participating teacher(s) are also the design team. Third, job-embedded learning is relevant to teacher's professional responsibilities. Fourth, principals can multiply themselves by implementing peer supervision. Fifth, job-embedded learning can provide principals time for their own learning.

Building Staff Development Time into the Regular School Day

Time for learning built into routine school days is needed, and the principal can consider two strategies for extending learning time into the regular school day by

- ♦ *rearranging existing time:* planning time for teachers is rearranged to create extended time for teacher learning and planning; and

- ♦ *creating additional time:* planning time, in addition to the traditional daily planning period, is provided for collaborative learning.

In the best of all worlds, teachers would have extended periods for collaborative planning and learning without having to sacrifice any of their traditional planning time. In the elementary arena, some principals have discovered that by multiplying the school site's workers through innovative use of outside volunteers, this dream can be realized. The varied and complex nature of the curriculum in the secondary arena creates an ideal setting for enlisting the assistance of outside experts. Since district and state attendance mandates as well as curricular requirements confine the frequency with which students may be released, schools can multiply their workers through volunteers to provide time for teacher learning. The key is the recruitment of enough volunteers to make release of the teaching faculty for a half-day or full day of learning and planning possible. Volunteers to support this effort can come from parents, patrons of the district, and local business and professional people, especially those who look to the local school district to produce the best possible workforce.

An Overview of Staff Development
Models that Link to Instructional Supervision

Each of these models contains elements of both instructional supervision and staff development. Often, staff development initiatives are motivated by data collected during classroom observations. In turn, various supervisory techniques can be used to collect data for assessing existing staff development initiatives and planning for future staff development needs. The value of these models is that they can be modified to fit the needs of teachers.

Peer Coaching

The origins of peer coaching, according to Showers and Joyce (1996), come "from two unlikely bedfellows—the world of athletics and research on the transfer of training—school districts are borrowing the concept of coaching to increase the effectiveness and acceptability of staff development" (p. 43). Peer coaching resembles the clinical supervision model and includes a pre-observation conference, an extended classroom observation, and a post-observation conference. Yet, peer coaching can extend the clinical model of supervision. A feature of peer coaching is to ensure the transfer of newly learned skills from an in-service (staff development) learning opportunity into practice. To this end, peer coaching is also used as a strategy to teach new instructional strategies to teachers. In this respect, peer coaching is a multifaceted tool that can simultaneously be used as an instructional strategy, a staff development strategy, and a complement to instructional supervision.

In peer coaching, teachers are able to observe one another at work, share strategies, engage in guided practice as follow-up to staff development, and reinforce learning through feedback, reflection, and ongoing inquiry. Through the feedback and collaborative problem solving during the post-observation conference, a new focus for the next observation can be formed.

Schools that support and nurture peer coaching promote leadership among teachers. Because there is no evaluation involved, peer coaching provides teachers with a nonthreatening way of having a "second set of eyes"—a colleague who can help facilitate learning through extended dialogues in both the pre-observation and post-observation conferences. Peer coaching provides motivation to study the existing literature on best instructional practice, the impetus to try implementing new practices, and feedback—symbolic of the natural linkage of staff development and instructional supervision.

The formal dialogue that occurs within a coaching relationship underscores the need for informal dialogue. Talking with colleagues about teaching helps break down the isolation created by the confines of classrooms. Informal dialogue also provides a forum completely devoid of value judgment so teachers are freed to share successes and difficulties in their practices.

Study Groups

The use of study groups is based on the discovery made by Joyce and Showers (1982) that outside experts are no more effective in offering feedback to teachers than teachers themselves. Study groups provide teachers a forum for dialogue, collaborative planning, and team building. According to Murphy and Lick (1998), groups should consist of four to six members. Although most study groups are formed across departments or teams, groups can also be homogeneous (e.g., all math or science) in membership. For study groups to survive, groups need

- a common belief system that supports the need for lifelong learning;

- administrative support such as release time and access to research; and

- a quality facilitator to keep meetings on track.

Action Research

Action research is a method of inquiry "undertaken by educators in order to better understand the education environment and to improve practice" (Grady, 1998, p. 43). Action research (undertaken by teachers) is research that occurs in conjunction, and often concurrently, with day-to-day classroom or school activities. Action research as an extension of instructional supervision can help teachers analyze their classroom practices. By integrating aspects of action research with processes of supervision, a more powerful and seamless form of learning emerges from such efforts.

Action research can broaden the clinical model of supervision by focusing attention more specifically on a practice or a dilemma the teacher wants to examine—over an extended period. Through inquiry, teachers become active learners who seek to make discoveries about their practices, and according to Dewey, "each day of teaching ought to enable a teacher to revise and better in some respects the objectives aimed at in previous work" (1929, p. 75).

Making decisions is a daily activity that teachers engage in as they interact both in and out of the classroom environment. Think of the number of split-second decisions a teacher makes throughout the course of teaching a lesson, interacting with students, and handling the "pop-up" situations that occur in the classroom. In split-second decision making, there is little time to stop, analyze, and reflect on the data that lead to making the decision. Good decisions are based on data. Better decisions are made after collecting and examining data, reflecting on alternatives, and getting feedback from another person.

Action research is one way in which teachers become "doers" through their own intentional actions of collecting, analyzing, reflecting, and then modifying practice. Extending the clinical supervision model to include action research is a doable option—if numerous cycles of the clinical model (pre-observation conference, extended classroom observation, and post-observation conference) are available to teachers. With the advent of peer coaching, peers can be involved in providing multiple cycles of coaching that mirror the clinical supervisory model. Glanz (1998) identifies four steps for conducting action research. These steps include:

- *Select a focus.* Decide what you want to investigate, what questions will help elicit the information needed, and design a plan to answer those questions.

- *Collect data.* Gather information, using tools such as Likert scale instruments, observations, interviews, criterion-referenced and norm-referenced tests, discussion/focus groups, school profile data (e.g., attendance statistics, discipline referrals), or portfolios.

- *Analyze and interpret data.* Use statistical tests on quantitative data and develop themes in qualitative data.

- *Take action.* Develop a plan of action based on the information collected and analyzed. (pp. 24–26)

The lessons learned from the results from action research in one area can lead to new avenues for teachers to investigate further. Teachers in schools in which action research is an integral part of staff development realize the power of action research—data inform practice.

Summary

Learning expends resources. Through a seamless approach of connecting supervision, staff development, and evaluation, the principal takes a step in the right direction of unifying efforts to promote teacher growth and development. To provide appropriate learning opportunities, the principal understands the career stages of teachers, the principles of adult learning, the vital importance of sustained "teacher talk" over time, and coaching. In addition to staff development conducted outside of school hours, teachers need learning opportunities that are a part of their daily work. Fulfilling this need requires time during the day. By providing learning resources for the school's most important human resource—teachers—principals can make a lasting investment in student learning. Through job-embedded learning techniques such as coaching, study groups, and action research, the principal situates teachers as the "doers" in their own learning.

Suggested Reading

Glanz, J. (1998). *Action research: An educational leader's guide to school improvement.* Norwood, MA: Christopher-Gordon.

Guskey, T. R. (2001). *Evaluating professional development.* Newbury Park, CA: Corwin Press.

Killion, J. (2001). *Assessing impact: Evaluating staff development.* Oxford, OH: National Staff Development Council.

Murphy, C. U., & Lick, D. W. (1998). *Whole faculty study groups: A powerful way to change schools and enhance learning.* Newbury Park, CA: Corwin Press.

Robb, L. (2000). *Redefining staff development: A collaborative model for teachers and administrators.* Portsmouth, NH: Heinemann.

Sparks, D., & Hirsh, S. (1997). *A new vision for staff development.* Oxford, OH: National Staff Development Council.

Zepeda, S. J. (1999). *Staff development: Building learning communities.* Larchmont, NY: Eye on Education.

4

Formal and Informal Classroom Observations

Instructional Leaders Conduct Informal and Formal Classroom Observations

In this Chapter . . .

♦ Intents and purposes of instructional supervision and evaluation

♦ Differentiated and developmental supervision

♦ Marginal teachers

♦ Informal and formal supervision

♦ The steps in the clinical model of instructional supervision

By statute and district policy, the principal is required to evaluate teachers. There is value to both supervision and teacher evaluation, and both need to be included in the overall effort to help teachers improve their instructional practices, to move toward increased student learning, and to realize the goals set forth in school improvement plans. Supervision and teacher evaluation do not need to be an either/or proposition—both supervision and teacher evaluation can coexist, and both of these processes can complement each other.

This chapter leads the principal through informal and formal supervision and evaluation to build a foundation for formal classroom observations, using the clinical model of supervision. The clinical model is a suitable one because it contains as a baseline the pre-observation conference, an extended classroom observation, and a post-observation conference. Effective supervisory practices are built on these processes.

This chapter also examines the marginal teacher and ways to work with teachers who are struggling to provide effective instruction. Working with the marginal teacher can be one of the most frustrating aspects of supervising the instructional program, but to avoid confronting marginal performance creates the conditions that promote mediocrity in students' learning. The stakes are too high to accept anything but the absolute best efforts from teachers.

Intents and Purposes of Supervision and Evaluation

Understand the History of Supervision, Evaluation, and Other Related Programs

The astute principal uses both supervision (formal and informal) and evaluation (formal and summative) to work with teachers. Before moving into the discussion of the intents of supervision and evaluation, the principal is encouraged to learn about the supervisory and evaluative practices in the building. This process will help the principal new to a building better understand why things are done a particular way. Knowing this information can prevent the newcomer from stepping on landmines and serve as a primer for looking at what is possible and practical.

- ♦ *Check district policies and procedures related to supervision and evaluation.* What are the "rules" and "regulations" relative to the number of observations, length of observations, and special requirements for tenured and nontenured teachers and for teachers on plans of improvement?

- ♦ *Investigate the history of supervision and evaluation.* This is especially important for a principal new to a school. Have there been grievances filed over unfair evaluation practices? What was the style of the last principal—informal, formal, or hands-off?

- ♦ *Understand the school's culture and climate.* Norms of collegiality—do teachers welcome administrators into their classrooms? Do teachers value feedback?

- ♦ *Examine the procedures of supervision in place.* Based on records, have teachers been engaged in full cycles of supervision including the pre-observation conference, an extended classroom observation, and the post-observation conference? If so, when do most cycles occur? At the end of the year, immediately before summative evaluations are due to central office? Throughout the year? After complaints from teachers, students, parents, or central office administrators?

♦ *Know who the players are.* Who beside the principal is involved with formal and informal supervision—assistant principals, department chairs, lead teachers, and/or instructional coordinators? Did the last principal supervise or evaluate only?

♦ *Look for linkages to other teacher support programs closely related to supervision.* Peer coaching, action research, mentoring and induction, and portfolio development are examples. If these programs exist, who supervises these programs? Who participates in these programs?

Instructional supervision aims to promote growth, development, interaction, fault-free problem solving, and a commitment to build capacity in teachers. When teachers learn from examining their own practices with the assistance of others, whether peers or supervisors, their learning is more personalized and therefore more powerful.

Formative Supervision and Summative Evaluation

The intents of instructional supervision are *formative:* concerned with ongoing, developmental, and differentiated approaches that allow teachers to learn from analyzing and reflecting on their classroom practices with the assistance of another professional (Glatthorn, 1990; Glickman, 1990). By contrast, the intents of evaluation are *summative:* classroom observations and other assessments of professional performance lead to a final judgment or overall rating (e.g., S = satisfactory, E = excellent, NI = needs improvement). McGreal (1983) made clear that all supervisory roads lead to evaluation, and supervisors cannot evaluate teachers until they have spent considerable time observing teachers *in* their classrooms.

Research on the practice of supervision reveals that most K–12 schools shortchange the original intents of instructional supervision by supplanting it with evaluation (Sullivan & Glanz, 2000). Supervision for the sake of evaluation does not support teacher growth and development.

The Intents of Instructional Supervision

The intention of supervision is to promote

♦ face-to-face interaction and relationship building between the teacher and supervisor (Acheson & Gall, 1997; Bellon & Bellon, 1982; McGreal, 1983);

♦ ongoing learning (Mosher & Purpel, 1972);

◆ the improvement of students' learning through improvement of the teacher's instruction (Blumberg, 1980; Cogan, 1973; Harris, 1975);

◆ data-based decision making (Bellon & Bellon, 1982);

◆ capacity building of individuals and the organization (Pajak, 1993);

◆ trust in the processes, each other, and the environment (Costa & Garmston, 1994);

◆ change that results in a better developmental life for teachers and students and their learning (Sergiovanni & Starratt, 1998).

Given the intents of supervision, principals attend to the varying needs of teachers by providing supervision that is differentiated and developmental in nature.

Differentiated Supervision

Glatthorn (1997) describes differentiated supervision as "an approach to supervision that provides teachers with options about the kinds of supervisory and evaluative services they receive" (p. 3). Differentiated supervision operates on the premise that teachers should have a degree of control over their professional development and the power to make choices about the support they both need and receive. According to Glatthorn (1990), teachers *must* be involved in at least two of the following:

◆ *Intensive development* (mandatory use of the clinical supervision model)

◆ *Cooperative development* (developmental, socially mediated activities such as peer coaching or action research)

◆ *Self-directed development* (developmental activities teachers direct on their own)

The differentiated approach is not meant to be prescriptive, but rather "a process approach, in which each school district or school develops its own homegrown model, one responsive to its special needs and resources" (Glatthorn, 1990, p. 179). Homegrown models include peer coaching, study groups, action research, and portfolio development. Teachers who participate in differentiated supervisory experiences with colleagues are generally tenured; they are beyond the probationary period. Teachers who are on plans of improvement are usually not involved in a peer-mediated, differentiated form of supervision.

The context of the school, the available resources, the experience level of teachers, and the school's culture serve as the design features of developing a differentiated supervision program. The principal needs to work with teachers to develop and nurture the norms of collegiality and trust needed for differentiated supervision to thrive. The principal also needs to ensure that teachers have the resources to engage in differentiated forms of supervision (time, training, materials). Finally, the principal needs to be involved in getting such initiatives started and know when to get out of the way so that teachers can own the program.

Closely related to differentiated supervision is the developmental approach (Glickman, 1981). In Chapter 3, aspects of teacher career stages and the basic principles of adult learning were explored; career stage theory and principles of adult learning are essential to developmental supervision.

Developmental Supervision

Glickman (1981) asserts that the "goal of instructional supervision is to help teachers learn how to increase their own capacity to achieve professional learning goals for their students" (p. 3), and a supervisor's style either enhances or diminishes teachers' abilities to engage in learning that is developmentally appropriate. The success of developmental supervision rests on the principal's ability to assess the conceptual level of the teacher or a group of teachers and then apply a supervisory approach (direct, indirect) that matches this level. Figure 4.1 highlights the commonalities of differentiated and developmental supervision.

Figure 4.1. Commonalities of Differentiated and Developmental Supervision

Differentiated and Developmental Supervision Promotes …

♦ The investigation of practice through experimentation, observation of others, and discovery.

♦ The determination of the type of supervision by the individual based on self-perceived needs.

♦ The teacher-as-learner situated as active participant in the experience of learning in the company of others through formulating hypotheses about practices, developing and testing alternatives in practices—action research.

♦ Interactions with others in constructing and reconstructing practices—lesson reconstruction.

♦ Nonjudgmental feedback and open exchanges with others.

♦ Self-directed learning.

The Intents of Teacher Evaluation

Teacher evaluation is summative and ideally occurs as a complement to formative supervision. The intents of evaluation are to meet state statutes and district policies, assign teachers a rating at the end of the year, and determine whether a teacher will return to work. The purposes of evaluation and supervision need not be in direct opposition; both can support the improvement of instruction. At the end of every quarter, semester, and school year, teachers assign students a final grade based on the work accomplished during that time. In the same vein, teacher evaluation leads to a rating for the year. Like students who receive input throughout the year, teachers receive input about their performance through professional activities such as multiple cycles of supervision and then receive an overall rating. The rating serves as a benchmark.

Much of the inherent conflict and tension between supervision and evaluation stems from the intent or outcome of evaluation. Acheson and Gall (1997) highlight the conflict between evaluation and supervision:

> One of the most persistent problems in supervision is the dilemma between (1) evaluating a teacher in order to make decisions about retention, promotion, and tenure, and (2) working with the teacher as a friendly critic or colleague to help develop skills the teacher wants to use and to expand the repertoire of strategies that can be employed. (p. 209)

Admitting an enduring struggle with the dynamics described above, Acheson and Gall argue that supervision and evaluation ultimately serve the same purposes and that "the improvement of instruction" (p. 48).

Given the hectic nature of the work of teachers and administrators, supervision and evaluation are often practiced as the same; a single classroom observation toward the end of the year yields an immediate rating. Most teachers experience evaluation as "a principals' report of teacher performance, usually recorded on a checklist form, and sometimes accompanied by a brief meeting" (Peterson, 2000, p. 18). Little wonder that teachers do not easily see the distinctions between supervision and evaluation.

McGreal (1983) suggests that when teachers receive their summative rating for the year—S, E, or NI—growth ceases. Perhaps a contributing factor is the variety of outcomes linked to teacher ratings—promotion, retention, termination, and pay raises. Peterson (2000) suggests 12 new directions for teacher evaluation that can bridge the stultifying gulf between supervision and evaluation:

♦ Emphasize that the function of teacher evaluation should be to seek out, document, and acknowledge the good teaching that already exists.

- Use good reasons to evaluate.

- Place the teacher at the center of evaluation activity.

- Use more than one person to judge teacher quality and performance.

- Limit administrator judgment role in teacher evaluation.

- Use multiple data sources to inform judgments about teacher quality.

- When possible, include actual pupil achievement data.

- Use variable data sources to inform judgments.

- Spend the time and other resources needed to recognize good teaching.

- Use research on teacher evaluation correctly.

- Attend to the sociology of teacher evaluation.

- Use the results of teacher evaluation to encourage the development of a personal professional dossier, publicize aggregated results, and support teacher promotion systems. (pp. 4–12)

Supervision can become "the heart of a good teacher evaluation system" (Acheson & Gall, 1997, p. 60).

Working with Marginal Teachers

In light of recent federal legislation raising the accountability bar even higher, successfully supporting the improvement of marginal teachers is of paramount importance. One of the most difficult tasks for a principal is working with a marginal teacher; however, the good news is that there are very few, about "5 percent of the teaching corps" (Peterson, 2000). A marginal teacher is one who manages to perform just well enough to keep his or her job to the detriment of student learning.

Lawrence, Vachon, Leake, and Leake's (1993) description of a marginal teacher focuses on lackluster instruction, and the assertion that "a marginal teacher is an individual who is consciously or unconsciously losing faith in the belief that every child can learn" (p. 5). They indicate that marginal teachers typically engage "in boring, uninspiring, and ineffective instruction. In unhealthy, toxic cultures, marginal teachers blame students for failure" (Deal & Peterson, 1999). Marginal teachers take their toll on students, teachers, and the community in which the school resides. Working with a marginal teacher requires skills in supervising and evaluating performance; working with a marginal teacher will take efforts away from working with other teachers; working with a marginal teacher diverts attention from school-based improvement efforts. Moreover, think of the marginal teacher at the high school level who teaches 150 students a year. The number of students a marginal teacher will teach in a 30-year career is 4,500 students. More than likely, this number is greater than the total enrollment of the entire school.

Fuhr (1990) identifies three general types of marginal teachers: (1) those with inadequate teaching skills, (2) those with personal problems, and (3) those with attitude problems. Dismissal, if it becomes necessary, is in the domain of the principal. For teachers with inadequate teaching skills, traditional supervisory processes and staff development strategies can help assist the marginal teacher to improve performance. In some cases, however, a specific plan of improvement that identifies skills to improve and strategies for achieving needed improvement is needed. The principal has the duty to supervise the plan of improvement, ensuring that the objectives associated with remediating the deficiencies are met to a satisfactory level of performance.

If the issue with a marginal teacher is a personal problem, the principal can enlist others who can provide a range of assistance (e.g., employee assistance program). When the personal issue is resolved, the marginal teacher's performance will usually return to an acceptable level (Fuhr, 1990). Perhaps the most difficult type of marginal teacher to assist is one with an attitude problem. If the attitude problem does not improve and dismissal becomes necessary, the principal must take the lead in the process.

Taking the lead in the dismissal process is a double-edged sword. On the one hand, teachers know who the marginal teachers are in the building. Competent teachers have little professional respect for marginal teachers, because they take away from the strength of the group. Parents and students make generalizations about the competency of all teachers based on their experiences with marginal teachers. Marginal teachers, because they are able to get away with substandard teaching, erode teacher morale, and if gone unchecked, competent teachers begin to lose faith in the administration and the system that allows marginal teachers to continue without remediation.

On the other hand, nothing will send shock waves through a school system more than when a principal confronts a marginal teacher. Often, the very teachers who may complain to the principal about the lack of performance of a marginal teacher will be the ones who will be listening to the marginal teacher "pop-off" about what a principal is doing to remediate the situation. In school cultures that promote learning and development and in which the principal has established trust, the marginal teacher will have an audience limited to the confines of the faculty lounge. However, it is unsettling when a teacher is put on a plan of remediation, and it is possible that other teachers will become stressed. Although teachers do not like to work in the company of marginal teachers, teachers will form a safety net around their members.

Markers of Marginal Teacher Performance

There are no absolute markers of marginal teaching; there are, however, patterns that mark ineffective (marginal) teaching from effective teaching competence. Lawrence, et al. (1993) report the indicators of marginal teaching include "disproportionate disciplinary referrals; excessive student failure; and numerous complaints from students, parents, and even colleagues in the building (p. 5). Sawa (1995) reports the work of Dennis (1990) that marginal teachers show excessive patterns across areas including:

- excessive lack of preparation;
- excessive deficiencies of teaching skills;
- excessive problems of student control;
- excessive manifestations of poor judgment; and
- excessive absence from school.

The principal must confront excessive behaviors. In the final analysis, the principal is accountable for the instructional program and all who deliver it. The principal who monitors the instructional program will have a frame of reference for the instructional (including classroom management) behaviors of the marginal teacher. This frame of reference can only be complete through first-hand knowledge gained through classroom observations, examination of artifacts (student referrals), and ongoing discussion with the marginal teacher.

What should a principal do once marginal teaching has surfaced? As Platt, Tripp, Ogden, and Fraser (2000) suggest—confront marginal teaching. They report that many principals prefer to play it safe, and they rely on other strategies, including transferring the teacher, moving high-maintenance students, and tailoring classes and the master schedule so the mediocre teachers does less harm. These are ineffective strategies in that the problem of lackluster teaching still exists, and the teacher is still marginal.

The principal must examine many aspects of the situation before proceeding, and this examination will take time. Some things that the principal should uncover include:

- *The teacher's history in the building and district.* How many years has the teacher been in the field? In the building? In the district? How many times has the teacher been transferred from one school to another?

- *What have prior reports on the teacher's performance indicated?* Are there areas that have been noted as unsatisfactory in the past, and what has been done to remediate these weaknesses?

♦ *What has brought to your attention this teacher's performance?* Student, parent, teacher, and/or central office complaints?

♦ *Outline the issues very specifically.* Mr. Jones's lack of classroom management skills interferes with students being able to learn. Mr. Jones has referred over 50 percent of his students to the assistant principal for coming to class unprepared and for not handing in homework. Nine parents have called requesting that their children be transferred from Mr. Jones's class; two teachers have complained that they have difficulties teaching near his classroom because of the noise; and the department chair has spoken with you about the situation. Informal classroom observations have yielded a long list of suggestions for Mr. Jones to consider related to his classroom management. Follow-up observations have yielded less than satisfactory implementation of suggestions.

♦ *What have you done so far to address the issues with Mr. Jones?* Who, beside you, have been involved in addressing these issues?

With a framework, the principal is in a more solid position to work with the marginal teacher, formally developing a plan of remediation with the intent of helping the teacher overcome weaknesses in classroom performance. Developing, implementing, and monitoring a plan of remediation (often called a plan of improvement or a professional development plan) is time intensive and requires an eye to detail. Depending on how things progress, a teacher on a plan of remediation may be recommended for termination.

The principal is encouraged to do three things before proceeding further.

1. *Study district policies and procedures* for the plan of remediation and develop a timeline according to the policies and procedures outlined in district documents. Examine the history of how the union or bargaining unit gets involved with personnel issues (grievances).

2. *Consult with your immediate supervisor* (a central office director) or the director of personnel who can give you guidance on how to proceed.

3. *Remember that issues of confidentiality* will prevent you from discussing the issues with anyone except your immediate supervisor, the director of personnel, or the superintendent, and possibly, legal counsel. This is important to remember in that the "grapevine" will circulate that a teacher is on a plan of improvement. Some teachers will want to affirm that you are doing the right thing, and some teachers will want to find out what is going on because of their allegiances with the marginal teacher.

Working with a Marginal Teacher—
Formal Plan of Remediation

The intent of any plan of remediation should be the growth and development of the teacher who is experiencing difficulty in the classroom. The intent is for the teacher and the principal to work as a team so that deficiencies can be removed. Sometimes this is easier said than done. When a principal observes consistent problems and patterns of behavior that interfere with student learning, it is time to move toward a formal plan of remediation. Most school systems have different levels of remediation from in-house to more intensive levels of remediation. Most plans of remediation include basic information found in Figure 4.2.

Figure 4.2. Components of a Plan of Remediation

1. Identification of the problem or areas of concern. A description of the areas of concern must be available. The description must also include artifacts that chronicle the areas of concern.

2. Communicating the problem or areas of concern to the teacher both orally and in writing.

3. Developing strategies to remediate the marginal performance. Strategies must be specific with the end in mind. Specific teacher behaviors must be specified with expected levels of performance included.

4. Timelines must be included in the plan of remediation: when the plan begins, the frequency in which the teacher's performance will be evaluated, and by whom.

5. Progress toward the goals of improvement must be documented. Both the teacher and the principal (and in the case where a school system includes others in the process) include reports on progress.

6. Documentation of the process of the plan of remediation, including meetings with the teacher, strategies offered, progress made (or lack of progress), resources offered to assist the teacher, and timelines.

The principal needs to be in a position to offer both assistance and, at the same time, to take corrective actions beyond the plan of improvement if the teacher has not made progress.

Informal and Formal Instructional Supervision

Effective principals need to work with teachers on a daily basis, and they do not wait to be invited into classrooms. Principals find opportunities to drop in for informal visits, in addition to the more formal, mandated classroom observations tied to evaluation. Effective principals constantly scan the learning environment, looking for ways to help teachers develop further, and they do this by getting out of the main office to monitor the pulse of the school.

Teachers want principals to be accessible—but not just by having an open-door policy or by walking the halls during passing periods. In short, teachers want principals to visit their classrooms, and it is the principal's responsibility to do so. Figure 4.3 outlines how a principal might approach the task of getting supervision out of the main office and into the classroom.

Regardless of type of observation (formal, informal, peer), supervisory practices are bound by the context of the school site, the culture and climate of the school, the characteristics of teachers and administrators, and the values that the school community embraces.

Informal Classroom Observations

Sometimes referred to as *pop-ins, walk-ins,* or *drop-ins,* informal classroom observations

♦ are brief, lasting approximately 10 to 15 minutes;

♦ can occur at the beginning, middle, or end of a period; and

♦ can happen at any time during the school day.

Informal observations are not intended to supplant formal ones; they do not include a pre-observation conference and often forgo the post-observation conference as well.

The principal conducts informal classroom visitations *not* to catch the teacher off guard or by surprise, *not* as *snoopervision,* and *not* to interrupt classroom activities. One administrator in the field carries a sign printed with "Just Visiting" while conducting informal observations to put teachers at ease and reduce the tendency of teachers and students to stop their work.

Informal observations are one way for principals to get to know their teachers. By taking the time to observe the work teachers do on a daily basis *in their classrooms,* principals can exert informed effort and energy to assist teachers beyond formally scheduled observations.

Informal observations do not necessarily include a post-observation conference, but principals can strengthen their relationships with teachers by communicating *something* about what was observed. Although face-to-face interaction with a teacher is the best way to do this, Figures 4.4 (p. 100) and 4.5 (p. 101) offer sample forms for written comments after an informal classroom observation. Perhaps the most important aspect of communicating what was observed in a

(Text continues on page 100.)

Figure 4.3. Getting Supervision Out of the Main Office

To create the conditions for effective informal and formal supervision, the supervisor needs to examine the history and context of instructional supervision in the school. Issues include

The framework of the clinical supervision process:

♦ What is the history of supervision and evaluation at the site?

♦ What are the experience levels and other defining features of the faculty?

♦ What is done with information collected before, during, and after the observation?

♦ At what time of year does the cycle (pre-observation conference, extended classroom observation, and post-observation conference) occur?

♦ Does the cycle continue with another round?

The intent of classroom observations:

♦ Why am I observing a particular teacher?

♦ How often do I observe teachers?

♦ What is the length of an observation?

♦ Do I observe certain teachers more than others?

♦ If so, what factors motivate me to do so?

The nature of the interaction:

♦ Do I merely report what I observed?

♦ Do I try to link other activities such as staff development to the supervisory process?

♦ Are post-observation conferences conducted? In a timely manner?

♦ Where are pre- and post-observation conferences conducted? (In the teacher's classroom? The main office?)

Figure 4.4. Sample Informal Observation Note

> Dear Mary,
>
> I enjoyed my informal observation on September 9 during your Honors English class. The overheads used to illustrate the proper uses of dependent clauses kept students focused on the common mistakes they made in their own essays.
>
> Clear directions kept students on task when they broke into small groups to proofread their essays. The small group size (3) kept *all* students engaged. Perhaps you might want to share these techniques with other freshman Honors teachers!
>
> Thanks, and I hope to see you at the faculty tailgate party tonight!

Source: Zepeda & Mayers, 2000. Used with permission

teacher's classroom is to be as specific as possible and to avoid platitudes such as "good job." Teachers will benefit more from specific information about their teaching, the ways in which they interact with students, or an approach used to deal with a classroom event. Timeliness is also important: Just like students, teachers respond to immediate feedback.

Figure 4.5 provides another example for sharing information from an informal classroom observation.

Some principals feel comfortable writing a few comments during the informal observation and leaving the comments with the teacher on the way out the door. By doing this, the principal is able to not only give immediate feedback but also reduce the stress level of the teacher who might be anxious about having a visitor in the classroom.

Special care must be taken to ensure that informal classroom observations do not become disruptive or send mixed messages to teachers. This is especially true if the principal is new or if informal classroom observations have not been conducted in the past. To ensure positive responses to informal classroom observations and foster an environment that supports them, principals need to take certain steps:

♦ Publish procedures for observations at the beginning of the year.

♦ Conduct informal classroom visitations regularly (one or two per week).

Figure 4.5. Sample Informal Observation Form

Teacher_____

Date _____ Time _____ Class Period _____ Subject _____

Number of students present _____

Students were:

☐ working in small, cooperative groups

☐ making a presentation

☐ taking a test

☐ working independently at their desks

☐ viewing a film

☐ other _____

Teacher was:

☐ lecturing

☐ facilitating a question and answer sequence

☐ working independently with students

☐ demonstrating a concept

☐ introducing a new concept

☐ reviewing for a test

☐ coming to closure

☐ other _____

Comments: Nancy:

☐ Students were working independently at their desks.

☐ The rearrangement of the room (desk, podium, and table) allowed you to work independently with students on their essays *and* to keep an eye on students working at their desks.

Perhaps you should hold the next freshman level meeting in your room so others can see your room arrangement.

Thanks for letting me visit your room and see the work you do to help our students become better writers. I appreciate your efforts.

Marcie Stiso

Source: Zepeda & Mayers, 2000. Used with permission

♦ Remind teachers to ask you in to see something new and innovative.

♦ Avoid using informal observation to check on a teacher when you have received complaints from parents or others.

♦ Know when to leave if you sense that a personal teaching moment is in progress (Zepeda, 1995).

Informal classroom observations at the start of the year can be especially beneficial for first-year teachers and teachers new to a school. The start of the year marks a period of transition, and the presence of a supervisor signals that teachers are not alone. Informal supervision can help principals assess what teachers need to thrive in the classroom.

In response to teacher retirements and shortages in critical subject areas, a school may well hire 15 or more teachers a year. With increased hiring, principals will need help in making informal classroom observations. If the school has more than one administrator, dividing informal observations among supervisors can offer a useful solution. Figure 4.6 provides an example of how supervisors can track informal observations.

Figure 4.6. Tracking Informal Observations

Teacher	Supervisor	Informal Observation	Formal Observation	Period(s)/ Time(s)	Follow-up
Adams	Schmidt	09/01	10/05	1 (8:15–8:30) 5 (11:10–11:20)	Cooperative learning grouping
Baker	Marlowe	11/08	03/20	1 (8:15–8:25) 1 (8:15–8:25)	Instructional pacing
Beatty	Linton	09/05 09/08 10/18 11/07	10/07; 10/14; 11/02; 12/05	1 (8:30–8:45) 3 (10:10–10:25) 1 (8:15–8:25) 6 (1:05–1:15)	Classroom management; beginning and ending of period procedures
Burton	Schmidt	09/07	10/31	1 (8:00–8:15) 8 (2:15–2:30)	Classroom management

By reviewing the record of informal classroom observations, principals can determine whether any teachers have been missed, whether observations are spread evenly throughout a portion of the school year or the day (indicated by period or time of the observation), and what follow-up has been or should be made. Principals can also look for patterns. For example, in Figure 6.6, Marlowe did not observe Baker at all for four months; Linton is balancing informal and informal observations. The principal should interpret these patterns in the context of the school and the characteristics of the teachers being supervised.

Formal Classroom Observations

During a formal classroom observation, the principal typically spends extended time in the classroom. For example, in the state of Georgia current legislation calls for formal classroom observations to last approximately 20 minutes, and in Illinois, many school districts require two or more formal observations of at least 30 minutes before an end-of-the-year rating can be issued. Common sense suggests that extended visits are needed if the observer is to get more than a snapshot of the classroom environment. Only extended classroom observations can provide teachers with detailed information about their teaching and interactions with students.

Regardless of its length, a formal observation requires a pre-observation conference and a post-observation conference. Why are these necessary? The answer is not simple, but its core is that omitting these steps makes the visit a waste of time for the principal and the teacher. A pre-observation conference allows the principal to walk into a classroom having knowledge about:

♦ learning objectives;

♦ lesson content;

♦ overall placement in the lesson or unit (beginning, middle, end);

♦ long-term plan; and

♦ students' ability levels, (e.g., perhaps the students were struggling with a concept, and this was a review for them).

In short, the information learned in the pre-observation puts the teacher and principal on the same proverbial page. Like a person walking into a movie theater 30 minutes late, the principal who walks into a formal observation without conducting a pre-observation conference has to guess where to focus attention, who the major players are, where the story line is going, and how earlier events have influenced the action. Without a pre-observation conference, the principal lacks the clarity, focus, and perspective that give meaning to what is observed.

This lack of knowledge, however, leads to a bigger problem. What will the principal and teacher talk about in the post-observation conference? How meaningful will notes be? The pre-observation conference readies the supervisor to collect data focused on an aspect of the lesson about which the teacher wants more information. The post-observation conference presents these data in a way that helps the teacher reflect about classroom practices. Teachers need and want opportunities to talk about their teaching—as McGreal states, "The more teachers talk about teaching, the better they get at it" (1983, p. 63)—but the talk must be based on objective data derived from a properly conducted classroom observation. There is no substitute.

The pre-observation and post-observation conferences will be explored in greater detail in subsequent chapters. The key point here is that a formal and extended classroom observation without pre-observation and post-observation conferences is a waste of time and effort for both the supervisor and the teacher.

Many new principals and other supervisors freeze at the thought of observing a class on subject matter they are not certified to teach or in an area they do not know and understand (e.g., physics, special education, drafting). Furthermore, classroom observation calls for skills other than subject-matter knowledge. Other sources of concern for supervisors faced with the task of talking about teaching with another professional include

- insecurity about capturing data in a fast-paced lesson in a way that will make sense;

- unfamiliarity with the processes of clinical supervision (perhaps because they were never supervised in this way); and

- insufficient knowledge of grade levels (elementary, middle, high school), the characteristics of students at a particular level, or a range of instructional practices.

The following guide for talking about teaching (Figure 4.7) has evolved from the author's work at the University of Oklahoma and the University of Georgia and with administrators in the field. The guide presents broad categories (e.g., knowledge of subject matter) and possible indicators reflecting activity within each category (e.g., relates content to prior and future information). The categories and the possible indicators offer a point of departure for supervisors seeking to capture the work of the teacher during the observation and frame thoughts while preparing for the post-observation conference. The supervisor may well add other indicators that reflect what was observed in the teacher's classroom.

The information in Figure 4.7 can also be used in the post-observation conference to help target the discussion about what was observed.

(Text continues on page 107.)

Figure 4.7. Criteria for Talking about Teaching

Criterion	Possible Indicators
Knowledge of subject matter	♦ Transfers content/concepts to everyday life. ♦ Relates content to prior and future information. ♦ Communicates content in a logical and sequential manner. ♦ Uses words and content appropriate to subject area and students' abilities. ♦ Demonstrates subject knowledge. ♦ Actively pursues lifelong learning especially in subject area.
Effectiveness of instructional strategies	♦ Cooperative learning. ♦ Demonstrations. ♦ Guided and independent practice. ♦ Modeling.Specific feedback.Appropriate wait time. ♦ Age-appropriate competition, inclusive of individuals and groups. ♦ Instructional methodologies include all learning styles.Multiple intelligences. ♦ Questions asked at multiple cognitive levels. ♦ Technology incorporated as an instructional tool.
Classroom management	♦ Routines are evident. ♦ Rules and procedures are posted.Rules and procedures are enforced. ♦ Beginning and ending class procedures are in place. ♦ Teacher monitors student behavior.Rewards and consequences are in place. ♦ Physical environment is conducive to orderliness. ♦ Teacher ensures a safe environment.

Variety of assessment methods	♦ Written, verbal, and nonverbal assessment may include
	  • tests/quizzes/written exams
	  • teacher observation
	  • participation
	  • portfolios
	  • feedback
	  • projects
	  • barometer, thumbs up/down—checking for continued understanding and application
	  • peer teaching
	  • homework

Criterion	Possible Indicators
	◆ Assessments are frequent.
	◆ Assessment instruments are teacher/student driven.
	◆ Accommodations are made for alternative assessments and individualized where needed.
	◆ Assessments are based on curriculum objectives.
High expectations for all students	◆ Teacher establishes expectations and communicates them by words and actions.
	◆ Gives varying opportunities for success.Encourages each student to function at an appropriate level.
	◆ Begins instruction at level of the learner and plans for cognitive growth.
	◆ Provides enrichment opportunities as well as remediation.
Teacher/student rapport	◆ Student centered.
	◆ Open climate.
	◆ Interactions with students are positive.
	◆ Teacher demonstrates tact, patience, and understanding, fosters growth in student self-esteem.
	◆ Uses specific praise.
	◆ Demonstrates enthusiasm.
	◆ Generates excitement for learning.
Technology	◆ Basic computer skills:
	• keyboardingcomputer applications (e.g., Word, Excel, Power Point, Internet, and E-mail)
	• record-keeping programs
	• required and supplemental programs in specific areas of expertise
	◆ Multimedia:
	• use of various media equipment (e.g., VCR, laser disk, overhead projector)
	◆ Integration of technology within subject matter
Communication	◆ Uses standard English in written and spoken communication.
	◆ Reflects all learning styles and levels of functioning
Gender, race, and culture	◆ Teacher is sensitive to students' cultural backgrounds and the effect on learning.
	◆ Communication (oral and written) is free of bias.
	◆ Female and male students are treated equally. Calling patterns and other practices reflect this.

The Clinical Supervision Model and its Components

The clinical supervisory model comprises the pre-observation conference, an extended classroom observation, and a post-observation conference. Figure 4.8 portrays the phases of the original clinical supervisory model.

Figure 4.8. The Phases of the Original Clinical Supervisory Model

Basic Phase	Cogan (1973)	Goldhammer, Anderson, and Krajewski (1993)	Acheson and Gall (1997)
Clarifying the supervisory relationship	Establishing the relationship		
Planning	Planning with the teacher Planning for the observation	Holding the pre-observation conference	Holding the planning conference
Observing	Making the classroom observation	Making the classroom observation	Making the classroom observation
Analyzing	Analyzing the teaching/learning process Planning the conference strategy	Making the analysis and planning strategy	
Conferencing	Holding the conference	Holding the supervisory conference	Holding the feedback conference
Evaluating	Doing renewed planning	Holding the post-conference analysis	

Source: Acheson & Gall, 1997; Cogan, 1973; Goldhammer, Anderson, & Krajewski, 1993.

The clinical supervisory model currently in use is much more streamlined than the original model, and the focus has shifted from the supervisor's leadership to the teacher's initiative and response. This view is more empowering; the teacher has a greater voice in the process and is in a better position to construct knowledge.

Although more streamlined, instructional supervision is still time-intensive, and supervisors face many dilemmas as they try to deliver a supervisory program that is responsive to the needs of teachers in their schools. The perennial struggle to find time for mandatory formal classroom observations and for informal classroom visits is exacerbated in schools where many teachers are in their first year or new to the system. Although no clear-cut solution to this problem can be applied across all school systems, many supervisors have found creative ways to make the most of available human resources and provide a supervisory program that centers on teachers' needs.

The following ideas offer a point of departure for identifying proactive measures to empower teachers while reducing the burden on principals. First, supervisors can cast the net wide, framing a comprehensive system that includes department chairs, lead teachers, instructional coordinators, and other school leaders as peer coaches and mentors. Although formal authority to evaluate teachers is vested in administrators, teacher leaders can multiply the impact of the administrators' efforts.

Other sources of supervisory assistance include district-level subject-area coordinators and directors who are specialists in areas such as special education, English, foreign language, social studies, health, and math. Second, supervisors must provide resources to train and support teachers who are willing to coach and mentor their colleagues, and this is especially true for marginal teachers, teachers new to the profession (alternatively certified teachers), and beginning teachers in the first year of teaching. The investment will yield rewards not only in the professional development of teachers, but also in the correlated gains in student achievement.

The next three chapters explore in depth the pre-observation conference, the extended classroom observation, and the post-observation conference. These form the baseline of all models of supervision (e.g., peer coaching, peer supervision, and the clinical model of supervision).

Summary

A strong instructional program is built on a variety of factors, including formal and informal supervision, a strong teacher evaluation system, and the ability to work with teachers who have a range of abilities—from the very excellent to the marginal. Instructional supervision can occur through formal or informal classroom observations. Informal classroom visits, although brief, are important to the program of instructional supervision. Teachers need feedback more than once or twice a year; informal classroom observations provide valuable opportunities for more frequent interaction between the supervisor and the teacher. However, informal classroom observations lose value if they are predicated on fault finding or triggered by an unfavorable report from a parent or colleague.

Supervisors new to a building would do well to determine the history of supervision before making informal classroom observations. At first, the school's culture might not support such interaction between teachers and their supervisors. It takes time to establish trust and build a culture that embraces informal observations.

Formal, scheduled observations include pre-observation and post-observation conferences that engage teachers in sustained discussion about their teaching. Optimally, teachers will participate in at least one formal and extended classroom observation each year. Keeping a log of observations by various school personnel (e.g., department chair, assistant principal, principal) helps the supervisor identify patterns and determine the instructional needs of particular teachers.

Effective supervisors take advantage of a range of opportunities to become involved in the instructional lives of their teachers. A purposeful combination of formal and informal observations will help build a culture that supports this path toward professional development and growth.

Suggested Reading

Acheson, K. A., & Gall, M. D. (1997). *Techniques in the clinical supervision of teachers: Preservice and inservice applications* (4th ed.). White Plains, NY: Longman.

Glatthorn. A. A. (1997). *Differentiated Supervision* (2nd ed.). Alexandria, VA: Association for Supervision and Curriculum Development.

Peterson, K. D. (2000). *Teacher evaluation: A comprehensive guide to new directions and practices.* (2nd ed.). Thousand Oaks, CA: Corwin Press.

Pajak, E. F. (1993). *Approaches to clinical supervision: Alternatives for improving instruction.* Norwood, MA: Christopher-Gordon.

Platt, A. D., Tripp, C. E., Ogden, W. R., & Fraser, R. G. (2000). *The skillful leader: Confronting mediocre teaching.* Acton, MA: Ready About Press.

Wiles, J., & Bondi, J. (1996). *Supervision: A guide to practice.* Columbus, OH: Merrill.

5

The Pre-Observation Conference

Instructional Leaders Conduct Pre-Observation Conferences before Formal Classroom Observations

In this Chapter ...

♦ Attributes of a pre-observation conference

♦ Focus and the pre-observation conference

♦ The Johari Window and the pre-observation conference

♦ How to prepare for the classroom observation

Given their fast-paced workday and myriad extracurricular activities (e.g., club moderator, member of the school improvement team), teachers rarely have time to talk with adults about their classroom practices. The pre-and post-observation conferences of the clinical supervisory model give teachers this valuable opportunity.

Acheson and Gall (1997) indicate that the supervisor's main responsibility is to serve as "another set of eyes," holding up the "mirror of practice" in which the teacher can examine specific classroom behaviors. Supervisors who collect stable data during the observation provide a clearer reflection. During the conference that precedes a formal classroom observation, the supervisor determines what kinds of data to gather. The supervisor can also use this time to cultivate the supervisory relationship and to learn more about the teacher's classroom. The pre-observation conference opens the door to the teacher's world.

Attributes of the
Pre-Observation Conference

During the pre-observation conference, teacher and supervisor establish the focus for the classroom observation. In talking about concerns or areas of practice, the teacher should take the lead (though the teacher's career stage naturally makes a difference here). This conversation supports decisions about what data will provide useful information for the post-observation conference and what tools the supervisor will use to gather those data. Ideally, the pre-observation conference

- strengthens the professional relationship between the supervisor and the teacher;
- is held within 24 hours of the observation;
- takes place in the classroom where the observation will occur;
- defines a clear focus for the observation, with the teacher taking the lead;
- gives the teacher the opportunity to "talk through" teaching; and
- illuminates the context, characteristics, climate, and culture of the classroom.

The pre-observation conference is the cornerstone for the observation, setting the stage for all that follows.

Most school systems have their own pre-observation form. The teacher might want to complete this form in advance, although the supervisor and teacher should work together to determine the focus during the conference. The pre-observation form presented in Figure 5.1 (pp. 113–114) can help the supervisor

- better understand the classroom during the extended observation;
- identify the focus of the observation; and
- get teachers to talk about their classroom practices.

Understanding the classroom environment and the teacher's instructional objectives positions the supervisor to collect the specific data that can help teachers understand the dynamics of their work.

For convenience, Figure 5.2 (p. 115) provides a blank pre-observation conference form, and Figure 5.3 (p. 116) shows a typical completed form.

(Text continues on page 117.)

Figure 5.1. Pre-Observation Conference Form

Teacher _____   Date _____

Grade/Subject _____   Observer _____

1. Learning Objectives
   - *Content:* What will the students learn?

   Ask the teacher to walk you through the lesson for the observation (this is sometimes called pre-planning, an original process in the first clinical supervisory model). Make sure that you understand what topics (subject matter) will be covered during the class you will be observing. The teacher should make clear the objectives for the class.

   - *Process:* What will instruction look and sound like?

   What will the teacher be doing and what will the students be doing? Probe the teacher to articulate a "cause-and-effect" between what he/she will be doing and what it is anticipated that students will be doing.

   What instructional strategies will be used?

   Ask the teacher to talk you through the method so that you understand it. Try to discover why the teacher has chosen specific instructional strategies. Probe so that you understand both the content and the instructional method.

   - *Resources:* What resources and materials will the teacher use throughout the lesson?

   With the advent of technology, teachers have a variety of equipment available to enhance instruction. Technology can serve both as a resource and as an instructional method.

2. Understanding the Classroom Environment

   Schools are diverse. It is not likely that every math teacher who teaches Algebra I follows the same plan. This part of the pre-observation form focuses on the *characteristics, culture,* and *climate* of the classroom learning environment.

   - *Characteristics of the learners:* What are the students like? Are students on an even playing field in relation to performances, motivational levels, and abilities? Are there students with special learning needs that require modifications in instructional or assessment of learning?

   - *Culture and climate:* How do you characterize the atmosphere in the room? Invite the teacher to talk about "how things are run," "the roles students assume in the learning process," "the ways students communicate with one another and you," "the levels of cooperation," "student attitudes," and "student behavior and hot spots."

3. Looking for Results

   This portion of the pre-observation focuses on how the teacher will determine whether objectives have been met, how the teacher monitors for learning and application of concepts, and what types of assessments will be used in the class or later.

- ♦ *Assessment:* What teaching behaviors assist you in assessing whether students are learning? Query the teacher to identify what students will be able to demonstrate and what artifacts (test or quiz grades, portfolio artifact, project, essay) will be used to demonstrate mastery.

4. Focusing for the Observation

- ♦ The focus is perhaps the most important aspect of the pre-observation conference. The focus allows the observer to

  - • "zoom" into the area in which the teacher wants objective data describing teaching behavior; and

  - • collect better data because the supervisor will know what type of *observation tool* to use to collect more stable data.

Source: Zepeda, 1995.

Figure 5.2. Pre-Observation Conference Form

Teacher _____   Date _____

Grade/Subject _____   Observer _____

1. Learning Objectives
   - *Content*: What will the students learn?

   - *Process:* What will instruction look and sound like?

   - *Resources:* What resources and materials will the teacher use throughout the lesson?

2. Understanding the Classroom Environment
   - *Characteristics of the learners:* What are the students like?

   - *Culture and climate:* How do you characterize the atmosphere in the room?

3. Looking for Results
   - *Assessment:*

4. Focusing for the Observation

Figure 5.3. Pre-Observation Conference Form

Teacher __Ms. Rita Sanchez__   Date __09/28/02__

Grade/Subject __3rd Grade__   Language Arts Observer __Ms. Connie Elliot__

1. Learning Objectives
   - *Content:* What will the students learn?

   Students will learn about the words *like* and *as* and how these words are used in similes to compare two things.

   - *Process:* What instructional strategies will be used?

   A mini-lesson on similes will begin with students working in groups of three finding the words like and as in the short story "Annie Goes to the Bank." Each group will prepare a list of the similes in the story. Each small group will share with the class the similes they found. Teacher will lead a whole-class discussion, asking students to describe the characteristics of the words found. Students will brainstorm aloud with the teacher in analyzing the characteristics of the comparisons used in the story. Students will be asked to write two paragraphs that contain similes.

   - *Resources:* What resources and materials will the teacher use throughout the lesson?

   The short story "Annie Goes to the Bank," poster-boards to write similes.

2. Understanding the Classroom Environment
   - *Characteristics of the learners:*

   Students range in ability from below grade level to above grade level. The class has 11 students. One student is partially deaf and sits close to the teacher.

   - *Culture and climate:*

   The classroom atmosphere is student centered, and the students are sensitive to the special needs of the partially deaf student. Generally, the students work well together in small groups, but they are still learning the social skills needed to work as a member of a group.

3. Looking for Results
   - *Assessment:*

   Quality of responses during the discussion of the similes found in the story. The teacher will monitor student participation in the small group. The teacher will assess student paragraphs for the similes they write; a follow-up discussion will include the presentation of the similes written by students in their paragraphs. Students will also read and proof each other's work before turning in the assignment to the teacher.

4. Focusing for the Observation

   Ms. Sanchez wants to focus on (a) the way she breaks students into groups; (b) the clarity of directions she gives to students; (c) the way she monitors students working in small groups; and (d) the transitions between class activities (e.g., small group work to large group sharing).

Focus and the
Pre-Observation Conference

Perhaps the most important feature of the pre-observation conference is the focus for the upcoming classroom observation. Why is the focus so important? This is a complex question with a multifaceted answer. The focus serves to

- ◆ promote dialogue between the supervisor and the teacher;
- ◆ help the teacher identify a growth area; and
- ◆ help the supervisor identify what concrete data to gather and what observation tools to use.

Who should direct the focus portion of the pre-observation conference? The teacher? The supervisor? Both? Opinions vary, and there are no universal truths. Ideally, the supervisor and the teacher mutually agree on a focus for the observation. Here are some guiding thoughts.

Teacher-Directed Focus

Teachers, as professionals—capable of thinking critically about instruction, students, curriculum content, and methods—are able to make informed decisions about the development of their practices and thus direct their own learning. The teacher can identify the observation focus area based on

- ◆ interest in a target area;
- ◆ perceived need to improve in a specific area;
- ◆ follow-up on staff development areas; and
- ◆ areas under construction (e.g., trying a new technique).

When the teacher assumes responsibility for directing the observation focus, the supervisor takes a more indirect tack, perhaps helping the teacher to flesh out an area of focus.

Supervisor-Directed Focus

The supervisor perceives a particular need and guides the teacher to focus on this target. Supervisors tend to take a directive approach with certain groups of teachers (such as first-year teachers or those on a plan of remediation). A supervisor-directed focus can certainly be positive and fruitful; however, teachers often feel greater autonomy when they have authority to determine the observation focus.

Regardless of who sets the focus, it must be realistic. If the focus is too broad, the supervisor and teacher will be unclear about the data to be gathered. If the focus is too ambitious, the observer will need to collect too much data scattered across too many areas. Return to Figure 4.3 for information. Has Rita Sanchez asked Ms. Elliot to focus the observation too broadly? If you were Ms. Elliot, would you try work with Rita to narrow the focus? If so, what approach would you take?

Negotiating Boundaries for the Observation Focus

Experience

First-year teachers might need guidance in developing the observation focus. Consider the following sequence:

- For the first formal observation, let the first-year teacher guide the focus with minimal input from the supervisor.

- Based on the first observation, exert more influence, if necessary, on the focus of the second formal observation.

- Link the focus of all subsequent observations to data from prior observations and the discussions in post-observation conferences.

Extenuating Circumstances

Teachers on formalized plans of improvement will need a more directed focus

- to remediate a particular deficiency within a certain time; or

- to comply with other policies and procedures specified by the board of education, the bargaining unit, or state statutes.

Implications about Focus and the Observation

The focus steers the observer through the steps of the observation:

- Identify the instrument to collect useful data that will, for example, portray teacher and student activities or words, classroom procedures, instructional methods (pedagogy), and classroom management strategies.

- Focus intently on instructional behavior(s), record events, and present the teacher with a rich portrayal of practice to discuss and analyze during the post-observation conference.

- Assist as the teacher identifies an area to examine in detail.

Teaching does not occur in a vacuum; unexpected incidents may unfold during the observation. The supervisor may well notice events that fall outside the focus and may choose to discuss them—but with caution. Trust is at stake. Letting unanticipated incidents clutter the post-observation conference can smack of "gotcha" tactics. Consider these questions:

- Did the incident (e.g., unruly students) completely overshadow all instruction or student activities?

- If the event (e.g., unclear or incomplete directions, lack of classroom routines) is not discussed, will the teacher continue to encounter problems?

- Is the teacher even aware of the incident (e.g., students were out of sight)?

- Will calling attention to the event diminish the teacher-supervisor relationship?

Fear to Focus

If you asked a group of teachers why they hesitate to ask their supervisors to focus on an area of concern, the answer would more than likely be fear—specifically, the belief that their supervisors are out to get them. This fear—now practically a tradition in Pre-K–12 schools—grows whenever a supervisor supplants supervision with summative evaluation that serves only to comply with state mandates. In *Supervisors and Teachers: A Private Cold War*, Blumberg (1980) concludes that clinical supervision is irrelevant in a teacher's professional life; rather, it has become merely an organizational ritual. The only way to combat this fear is to build trust—trust between teachers and supervisors.

The Johari Window and the Pre-Observation Conference

Teachers may hesitate to admit a weakness—especially if they have experienced evaluation as supervision, have not engaged in open, fault-free discussions, or fear that their jobs are on the line. However, many teachers will ask for help—if they know they need it, and especially if they believe their supervisors will provide useful insight and resources.

One tool for exploring communication between supervisors and teachers is the Johari Window, developed by Luft and Ingham (1955) at the Western Training Laboratory. The Johari Window describes personal knowledge and interactions in terms of four panes: the open pane, the hidden pane, the blind pane, and the unknown pane. According to Luft and Ingham, the open pane and the hidden pane represent aspects of a person known to the self; the blind pane and the unknown pane represent aspects unknown to the self. Further, the open pane and the blind pane represent aspects known to others; the hidden pane and the unknown pane represent aspects unknown to others.

The Mallan Group Training and Management, Inc. (Tucson, Arizona), developed the Disclosure/Feedback model (Figure 5.4) to help people assess awareness of communication patterns using the principles of the Johari Window.

Figure 5.4. The Johari Window

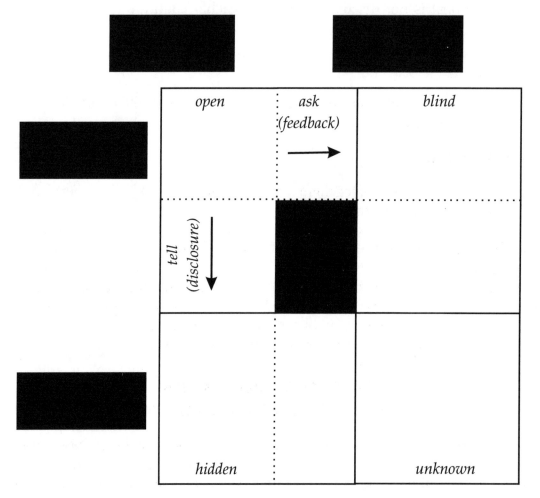

Source: Mallan Group Training and Management, Inc. KnowMe™. Retrieved May 30, 2001 from http://www.knowmegame.com/Johari_Window/johari_window.html. Used with permission.

The Mallan Group describes the four panes of the Johari Window as follows:

1. *Open.* The open area is that part of our conscious self—our attitudes, behavior, motivation, values, way of life—that we are aware of and

that is known to others. We move within this area with freedom. We are "open books."

2. *Hidden.* Others cannot know our hidden area unless we disclose it. Some aspects we freely keep within ourselves; others we retain behind a "closed" window out of fear. The degree to which we share ourselves with others (disclosure) is the degree to which we can be known.

3. *Blind.* There are things about ourselves that we do not know but others can see more clearly, or things we imagine to be true of ourselves for a variety of reasons but others do not see at all. When others say what they see (feedback) in a supportive, responsible way, and we are able to hear it, we can test the reality of who we are and open ourselves to growth.

4. *Unknown.* We are richer and more complex than the aspects we and others know, but from time to time something happens—is felt, read, heard, dreamed—that reveals something from our unconscious. Then we "know" what we have never "known" before.

(Used with permission of the Mallan Group Training and Management Inc).

The known and unknown sides of a person affect communication, the ability to be open to feedback, and the willingness to recognize a weakness or an area that is not readily known to the person.

Implications for Supervision

Supervisors can use the Johari Window to consider how teachers feel about being observed and to interpret what teachers say or do not say in the pre-and post-observation conferences. While working with teachers to frame a focus for the classroom observation, for example, the supervisor may be asking them to disclose a weakness that lies behind the hidden pane. Likewise, after the observation, the type of feedback chosen—and its intensity—will depend on how much teachers already know about their practices. (The discussion of the Johari Window will continue in Chapter 7, which addresses the post-observation conference.)

Teachers who are comfortable with their Johari Window need very little prompting to identify a focus for the classroom observation. Teachers with little experience—first-year teachers or those unfamiliar with the intents of supervision—might be more reluctant. The supervisor's job is to coach teachers in this aspect of professional growth.

The Open Pane

Some teachers are (or appear to be) very open when discussing their teaching, readily sharing both the triumphs and the trials of their efforts in the classroom. Such teachers often are willing to have others (teachers, supervisors) visit their classrooms to observe, gather ideas, and give feedback. These visits are good learning opportunities—*if* the teacher is indeed effective. However, such classroom observations could be disastrous if the teacher's practices and self-image are not congruent.

The Hidden Pane

Teachers who operate mainly in the hidden or secret part of the window say little about what goes on in their classrooms. Their reticence arises not from incompetence, but from insecurity or fear of not meeting expectations. The supervisor's job is to coach teachers into talking about their work. One approach is to engage the teacher in a general discussion of classroom practices and the learning objectives for a particular lesson. From this platform, the supervisor can guide the conversation with more specific questions. As trust develops between the teacher and supervisor, the discussion will arrive at a focus that the teacher wants to explore. It may take time to discover—or even uncover—what really matters.

The Blind Pane

We do not always see ourselves as others see us. The supervisor at the back of the room may observe an aspect of a teacher's classroom practices that needs attention, though the teacher is unaware of it. Bringing such aspects into the open can be a difficult task, especially if the teacher resists recognizing or acknowledging them. However, teachers may also be blind to their own strengths (though such news is usually welcome). In framing effective feedback, the supervisor should rely on objective data gathered during the observation.

The Unknown Pane

The unknown pane is the most difficult for people to open. This area hides information that only the individual can discover, in ways as individual as the person. Reflection, disclosure, and feedback can lead to this discovery, freeing the potential that lies behind the unknown pane. This aspect of the Johari Window offers perspectives that apply particularly to the post-observation conference, discussed in Chapter 7.

Prepare for the Classroom Observation

The primary tool for the pre-observation conference is some type of pre-observation conference form (see Figures 5.2 and 5.3). However, conducting a classroom observation requires other preparation as well. Effective supervisors arrive at the teacher's classroom ready to work. Here are some additional tools they use for an extended classroom observation.

Familiarity with the Teacher's Classroom

One way to become familiar with the classroom environment is to hold the pre-observation conference in that classroom.

Establishment of Boundaries

Effective supervisors enter the classroom without disrupting the class. During the pre-observation conference, the teacher and supervisor agree on the details: when and how to enter, where to sit, how long to stay, and how to leave. These boundaries frame the observation and put the teacher at ease.

Artifacts

In addition to paper and pencil, the prepared supervisor brings relevant artifacts such as instructional materials (handouts, textbooks) or multiple copies of the teacher's seating chart (an effective way to track calling patterns or chronicle other events).

Tools

One supervisor might use a laptop computer to track data related to the focus of the observation. Another might record events with a video camera. Using technology in classroom observations requires special care. For example, many school systems require parent permission to videotape children. Other district policies or union agreements might regulate videotaping teachers. Prospective and practicing supervisors need to be aware of district policies governing informal and formal observations, acceptable pre-and post-observation forms, and the method of communicating what they observed. To establish and maintain credibility with teachers and central administrators, the supervisor must know the school system's policies and procedures.

Summary

The formal supervision process includes the pre-observation conference, the extended classroom observation, and a post-observation conference. During the classroom observation, the supervisor's responsibility is to collect accurate, objective data that reflect events. (As Sergeant Friday used to say on *Dragnet*, "Just the facts, ma'am.") These data underpin the teacher's reflection and growth during the post-observation conference and beyond.

The pre-observation conference can be a learning opportunity for teachers; successful conferences promote dialogue about teaching, with the teacher in the lead. The supervisor's goal should be to extend the dialogue by asking questions that invite reflection and further analysis. Actively planning instruction in company with the supervisor can enhance the teacher's learning. The supervisor also learns—about the teacher, the students, and the upcoming lesson. A key component of the pre-observation conference is determining a focus for the classroom observation. In a sense, the focus serves as a guide for the teacher and the supervisor; it positions the supervisor to collect useful data for the teacher to analyze later.

In developing the focus of the classroom observation, the teacher opens one or more panes of his Johari Window. How much teachers disclose about their practices during the pre-observation conference depends on their experience and the degree of trust between supervisor and teacher. Effective supervisors are proactive; they encourage teachers to look deeply at their practices with an eye to improvement and further development. The pre-observation sets the stage for the classroom observation. The next chapter details the classroom observation and the tools that a supervisor can use to collect data.

Suggested Reading

Acheson, K. A., & Gall, M. D. (1997). *Techniques in the clinical supervision of teachers: Preservice and inservice applications* (4th ed.). White Plains, NY: Longman.

Thompson, D. P. (1996). *Motivating others: Creating the conditions.* Larchmont, NY: Eye on Education.

6

The Classroom Observation

Instructional Leaders Use a Variety of Tools to Collect Stable Data During Classroom Observations

In this Chapter ...

♦ The intents of data collection

♦ Types of data

♦ Wide- and narrow-angle data collection techniques

♦ Tips from the field

♦ Overview and application of observation tools

The pre-observation conference underpins the formal classroom observation. It provides an opportunity for teachers to talk about teaching, but more crucially, to identify a focus for the upcoming observation. The focus guides the supervisor's choice of a data collection tool. The quality and quantity of the data collected, as well as how the supervisor presents them, will significantly influence the quality of the post-observation conference.

Many tools and techniques allow the supervisor to collect stable, informative data in a systematic way. The supervisor, with input from the teacher, chooses one or more of these. At the end of the classroom observation, the key question is, "Do these data make sense?" Supervisors and teachers who invest time and effort in learning to use a variety of data collection tools can anticipate a rich return.

The Intents of Data Collection

According to McGreal (1983), data collection has four intents. Figure 6.1 outlines the intents of data collection during each phase of the clinical supervision model.

Figure 6.1. Data Collection Intents in the Phases of the Clinical Supervision Model

Clinical Supervision Phase	*Data Collection Intent*
Pre-observation conference	The reliability and usefulness of classroom observation is related to the amount and type of information supervisors have before the observation.
Pre-observation conference and extended classroom observation	The narrower the focus supervisors use in observing classrooms, the more likely they will be able to describe the events related to that focus.
Extended classroom observation	The impact of observational data is related to the way the data are recorded during the observation.
Post-observation conference	The impact of observational data on supervisor-teacher relationships is related to the way feedback is presented to the teacher.

Source: McGreal, 1983.

Implications for Supervisors

These intents can guide the supervisor not only in collecting data during the observation but also in framing discussions during the pre-and post-observation conferences. Supervisors need to work at collecting reliable data, free of value judgments and speculation. Consider the following two statements:

- *Statement 1:* "While you were giving instructions for the small-group activity, one girl left her seat to sharpen a pencil."

- *Statement 2:* "Because you were incapable of holding the students' attention, one girl sauntered to the pencil sharpener. From the smile on the girl's face, I believe she was mocking your shotgun approach to giving instructions."

The first statement presents the facts without editorial speculation. The second statement is value-laden; even its wording ("incapable," "sauntered," "shotgun approach") sends a negative message. How is the teacher likely to respond to each statement? What impact might the second statement have on the relationship between the supervisor and the teacher?

The primary objective of collecting data is to promote teacher analysis, reflection, and ongoing planning. The classroom is a complex setting, but the focus established in the pre-observation conference positions the supervisor to collect data that will make sense to the teacher. What technique will yield data that shed light on the focus? Figure 6.2 outlines the possibilities.

Figure 6.2. Classroom Observation Data Collection Methods

Method	Description
Behavior category	A narrow set of behaviors is determined and then tracked. Focus is more on the teacher than on the student.
Checklist	Supervisor uses a standardized form to identify activities and/or behaviors as present, absent, or in need of improvement. (Often disparagingly called "pencil whipping.")
Classroom diagramming	Supervisor tracks and records certain behaviors or movement of teachers and students in short increments of time.
Selected verbatim notes	Supervisor records words, questions, or interactions exactly.
Open narrative	Supervisor takes anecdotal notes, with or without a focus.
Teacher-designed instrument	Teacher develops an instrument to audit certain teaching and/or learning behaviors.
Audiotape	Teacher and/or supervisor can audiotape classroom events and listen to them later.
Videotape	May require the assistance of another person. Teacher can review the lesson alone or with a supervisor or peer.

Types of Data

Data may be quantitative, qualitative, or a combination of both. Quantitative data include frequencies, distributions, and other counts or tallies of information. Checklists are quantitative, because they do not use words to describe what occurred, how, or why.

For example, the observer could use a checklist to tally how many questions were asked of children in the front row, or how many times the teacher called on students whose hands were raised and those whose hands were not raised. Quantitative data have strengths; consider the following scenario.

In the post-observation conference, Mr. Cranston tells Mr. Jones, "During the first 10 minutes of class, you didn't call on any students in the first row." Mr. Jones, who thought his lesson went smoothly, responds with consternation, "I can't believe I could have completely ignored the whole front row!" However, Mr. Cranston has used multiple copies of the seating chart to track calling patterns in 10-minute increments. He invites Mr. Jones to examine the page for the first 10 minutes of class (see Figure 6.3).

Other classroom observation data may be qualitative. Qualitative classroom observation would include the scripted notes of the supervisor or peer coach. Figure 6.4 (p. 130) shows an example of qualitative observation data.

Figure 6.3. Quantitative Data Sample

Date: 12/21/03   Beginning Time: 8:15   Ending Time: 8:45
Teacher: Mr. Martin Jones   Observer: Mr. Adam Cranston
Lesson Topic: Fractions   Grade/Level: Grade 7
Date of Post-Observation Conference: 12/22/03 (after school)

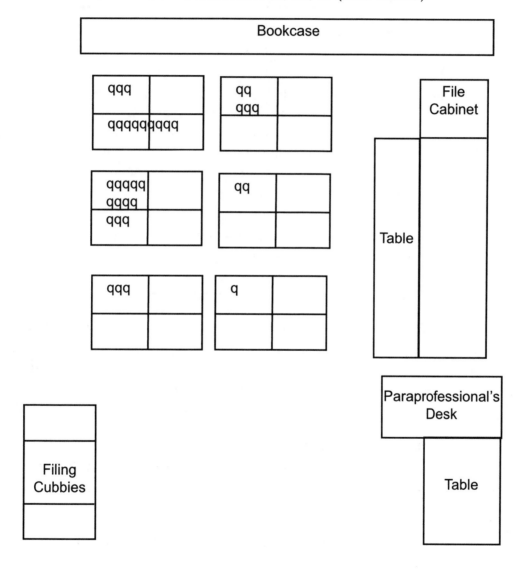

Applying Concepts

♦ If you were Mr. Cranston, how would you approach getting Mr. Jones to see the data as portrayed in Figure 6.3?

♦ In what ways did the data make the observation more credible?

Figure 6.4. Qualitative Data Sample

Date: 09/07/03   Beginning Time: 8:15 Ending Time: 8:45
Teacher: Mr. Jack Eliason   Observer: Mr. Oliver Campbell
Lesson Topic: Subject-Verb   Grade/Level: Grade 9
Date of Post-observation Conference: 09/29/03 (before school)

10:10:	T (teacher) asks Marcie to repeat the question. Marcie repeats: "What is the subject?"
10:11:	T: "Dog." "Ask 'who' or 'what' of the verb."
10:11:	T writes sentence on the board: *After the storm, several students left the roller rink.* T: "Try to ask 'wh' or 'what' against the verb, 'left.'"
10:13:	T: "Marcie, answer silently the question, 'Who left the rink?'" Marcie stares at the sentence on the board. Two students raise their hands; 3 students write on paper; 3 students in back reading grammar book; 5 other students speaking with one another.
10:16:	Marcie blurts out, "several left."
10:17:	T: "Go back to the sentence, examine the word 'several'—check to see if the word is an adjective, 'How many students?'"
10:18:	Marcie, "several—it's an adjective."

Although qualitative data record information in words, the patterns of activities, words, and other events observed and then recorded offer insights about the classroom environment. Whether data are quantitative or qualitative, accuracy is essential; the credibility of the process and the supervisor is at stake.

What Would *You* Do?

Consider the qualitative data in Figure 6.4.

♦ What patterns do you notice?

♦ What would you communicate to Mr. Eliason?

♦ As a supervisor, what would you want Mr. Eliason to discover about this teaching segment?

Look again at the dates of the classroom observation and the post-observation conference.

♦ How does the time lapse affect the effectiveness of the data?

♦ Would the effect be different if the data were quantitative?

Even in the qualitative report in Figure 6.4, certain observations can be quantified. For example, Mr. Eliason interacted for eight minutes with only one student (Marcie), while other students were off task.

Wide-angle and Narrow-angle Data Collection Techniques

Data collection may focus on a single aspect (or a few aspects) of instruction (e.g., specific types of questions the teacher asks) or on a wide range of circumstances in the classroom (e.g., how things are going in general). Acheson and Gall (1997) developed a series of data collection techniques that they categorize—in analogy to camera lens attachments—as wide-angle or narrow-angle tools. Wide-angle techniques allow the supervisor to capture a large picture; narrow-angle techniques "zoom in" to collect data focused on a single aspect or two.

For example, if a teacher asked the supervisor to focus on the types of questions asked of students, the supervisor might decide to record, verbatim, the questions asked—a narrow-angle technique. The supervisor could expand the lens to track student responses as well; this decision would be a judgment call based on the level of trust between the teacher and the supervisor.

A Case Study

Mrs. Ortiz, a first-year assistant principal, is in Mr. Martin's classroom observing a lesson on subject-verb agreement. The focus they agreed on in the pre-observation conference was to track calling patterns. Specifically, Martin wanted to know if he favored any students over others or called on students evenly to answer questions.

About 15 minutes into the observation, a few students in the front of the room begin talking and swapping what appear to be their lunch bags. Mrs. Ortiz stops collecting data on Mr. Martin's calling patterns; instead, she takes notes on these students and what they are doing.

At the end of class, Mrs. Ortiz returns to her office to review the classroom observation. She sees that almost half her notes deal with the students who were off task, swapping lunches with each other.

♦ How should Mrs. Ortiz handle this situation?

♦ What factors should guide Mrs. Ortiz in making her decision?

Figure 6.5 summarizes the six most commonly used data collection tools developed by Acheson and Gall (1997). In conjunction with the Association of Supervision and Curriculum Development (ASCD), Keith Acheson developed a videotape series that provides a detailed explication and examples of applying the tools based on video clips of teachers in their classrooms. More information is available at http://www.ascd.org/.

**Figure 6.5. Data Collection Tools:
An Overview of Types**

Type of Lens	Method to Collect Data	Focus
Narrow	Selective verbatim	Records words that were actually said by the teacher or the students.
Narrow	Verbal flow	Details the frequency of who spoke—how often and when.
Narrow	Class traffic	Tracks the teacher's (or students') physical movement.
Narrow	Interaction analysis	Provides detail about the types of statements made by either the teacher or the students.
Narrow	At-task	Provides detail, noting periodically over time what appears to be at-task.
Wide	Anecdotal notes	Notes overall what was occurring in the classroom. This can become more judgmental unless the supervisor records "Just the facts, Ma'am."

Source: Adapted from Acheson & Gall (1997).

Whichever method of data collection the supervisor chooses, it is a good idea to record major events such as teacher questions and student responses in detail. A few strong examples with complete and accurate information will make more sense for both the teacher and the supervisor than a long record of unfiltered information.

Tips from the Field

After the pre-observation conference, the supervisor should take time to plan for the observation and its immediate aftermath. Each extended classroom observation offers a valuable opportunity; effective supervisors learn to make the most of it. Attention to details at this point will pave the way. The tips listed in Figure 6.6 can assist the supervisor before, during, and after the classroom observation.

Figure 6.6. Tips from the Field

Before the observation	♦ Make 15 to 20 copies of the seating chart. Several techniques for observing student and teacher behaviors make use of the seating chart. Advantages: • A lot of information fits on a single chart. • The supervisor can record individual student behavior while observing the teacher and the class as a whole. • To track the observation in five-minute increments, turn to a new chart every five minutes. (It is easy to get five minutes' worth of data on a single seating chart). Examples of data that can be recorded easily on a seating chart: • Student/teacher question patterns • Reinforcement and feedback • Classroom movement
During the observation	♦ Start small—focus on observing one or two items, and take notes that relate directly to the focus identified during the pre-observation conference. ♦ Arrange to arrive a few minutes before class begins to have materials ready (laptop plugged in, video recorder set up).
After the observation	♦ Set aside time immediately afterwards to organize notes and thoughts. ♦ Send a note to thank the teacher for sharing the classroom experience. ♦ Secure resource materials (if applicable) related to the focus. Materials could include professional journal articles, videos, or staff development descriptions.

A Case Study

Judith Nile, principal at Richards Elementary School, had arranged to observe Rita Newman, a third-grade teacher, from 10:00 to 10:45 on a specified date. At 9:30, a fight broke out, and four students reported to the office. Ms. Nile dropped everything to deal with the incident. As a result, she did not show up for the scheduled observation. Later in the day, Ms. Newman tried to see Ms. Nile, but Ms. Nile was away at a district-level meeting for the rest of the day. Ms. Newman was upset.

♦ If you were in Ms. Nile's position, what would you have done and why?

♦ Dig deep and identify the issues operating in the case study.

Overview and Application of Observation Tools and Methods

A tool is useful only if the worker knows how to use it. Mastery comes with practice over time. The next section of this chapter details 10 tools that can help supervisors, peer coaches, and teachers as they track data from classroom observations. To illustrate their application, the description includes:

♦ an explanation of the tool and technique;

♦ a scenario introducing the teacher and the context of the classroom;

♦ an observation focus;

♦ the tool that would be appropriate for the observation;

♦ directions for using the tool;

♦ data collected from the observation; and

♦ suggested post-observation strategies and a discussion of the strategies.

These tools and methods offer a point of departure; feel free to revise these forms or develop your own to reflect the context of your classroom observations. In short, exercise your imagination to expand your toolbox.

Tool 1: Observation Guide for Using Bloom's Taxonomy

Teachers spend a great deal of time talking with students—lecturing, giving directions, and asking and answering questions. To ensure understanding and application of knowledge, teachers commonly engage students in question-and-answer sessions (known in the field as Q & A). Questions can prompt responses ranging from simple recall of information to abstract processes of applying, synthesizing, and evaluating information. Bloom (1956) developed a continuum for categorizing questions and linked this continuum to the application of objectives—behavioral, affective, and psychomotor. Bloom's Taxonomy frames the analysis of both written and oral questions. Figure 6.7 provides an overview of Bloom's Taxonomy of cognitive questioning. Note that the continuum represents thinking from lower-order to higher-order thinking. The information provided in Figure 6.7 offers a framework within which the supervisor can guide a teacher in analyzing questions.

Mrs. Anna Stevens, a third-grade teacher, is seeking feedback on the types of questions she asks while teaching fractions and decimals. Although Anna is a veteran teacher (15 years at the same school), until this year she taught first grade. During the pre-observation conference, Anna expressed concern that her questions might be too "elementary."

Observation Focus

Anna Stevens and her supervisor, principal Donald Taylor, agree that the classroom observation focus will center on the level of thinking skills elicited by the questions that Mrs. Stevens asks of her students.

Observation Tool

Mr. Taylor explains to Mrs. Stevens that he will use a data collection method called Selective Verbatim. Using the form shown in Figure 6.8 (p. 138), he will record only the questions Mrs. Stevens asks.

Directions

Write the sentence in the left-hand column. Put a check in the box that best describes the cognitive level of the question. (This may be part of the post-observation conference.)

(Text continues on page 139.)

Figure 6.7. Bloom's Taxonomy

Bloom's Taxonomy and Definition	Sample Question	Sample Verb Stems	Students' Responses Indicate Skills Such As
Lowest Order			
Knowledge/Recall: Students are asked to remember information.	Students answer questions that ask: Who, what, when, where, how … ? ♦ What is a fraction? ♦ Who created the smallpox vaccination? ♦ Describe the characteristics of the painting on page 24 of your book.	Summarize, describe, interpret	♦ Remembering. ♦ Memorizing. ♦ Recognizing. ♦ Identifying. ♦ Recalling.
Comprehension: Student demonstrates that he/she has sufficient understanding to organize and arrange material.	Students retell and organize events in a sequential order. ♦ After watching the film *Romeo and Juliet,* develop a sequence of events leading to the deaths of Romeo and Juliet.	Classify, discuss, explain, identify, indicate, locate, report, restate, review, translate	♦ Interpreting. ♦ Translating from one medium to another. ♦ Describing in one's own words. ♦ Organizing and selecting facts and ideas.
Application: Students apply previously learned information to reach an answer to a different but similar problem.	Students solve a problem or show a cause-effect relationship between similar items, events. ♦ How is the destruction of the World Trade Center similar to the bombing of the Murrah Federal Building?	Apply, choose, demonstrate, dramatize, employ, illustrate, interpret, operate, practice, schedule, sketch, solve, use, write	♦ Solving problems. ♦ Applying information to produce an end product.

Bloom's Taxonomy and Definition	Sample Question	Sample Verb Stems	Students' Responses Indicate Skills Such As
Analysis: Students critically examine events and perform certain operations such as separating whole to part or part to whole.	Students extrapolate motives and/or causes and draw conclusions. ◆ Why was there a dip in the economy after the September 11, 2001, attack on the World Trade Center?	Analyze, calculate, categorize, compare, contrast, criticize, differentiate, discriminate, examine, question, test	◆ Subdividing. ◆ Finding, identifying, and separating a whole into parts.
Synthesis: Students produce an original work, make predictions, and/or solve problems.	After analyzing the events of September 11, 2001, develop five recommendations for national security.	Arrange, assemble, collect, compose, construct, create, design, develop, formulate, manage, organize, plan, prepare, propose, set up, write	◆ Creating an original product.
Highest Order			
Evaluation: Students answer a question that does not have an absolute answer, provide an educated guess about the solution to a problem, or render a judgment or opinion with backup support.	What is needed to develop tolerance?	Appraise, argue, assess, attach, defend, judge, rate, support, value, evaluate	◆ Making a decision. ◆ Prioritizing information. ◆ Drawing a conclusion.

Source: Adapted from Allen, 2001; Barton, 1989; Bloom, 1956; Bloom's Taxonomy as described on websites of Counseling Services, University of Victoria; and Distance Learning Resources Network (DLRN).

Figure 6.8. Observation Guide for Using Bloom's Taxonomy

Date: 04/16/03   BeginningTime: 10:10 Ending Time: 10:30
Teacher: Mrs. Anna Stevens   Observer: Mr. Donald Taylor
LessonTopic: Fractions/DecimalsGrade/Level: Grade 3
Date of Post-Observation Conference: 04/16/03 (after school)

		Knowledge	Comprehension	Application	Analysis	Synthesis	Evaluation
				Levels of Thinking			
Time	Questions, Activities						
10:10	How many have heard the word decimal?	✔					
	What do you think decimals mean?	✔					
	How do you know?	✔					
	Have you ever seen a decimal?	✔					
	What do you think that means?	✔					
	Why the decimal? Why that period?	✔					
10:15	Decimal points do what?	✔					
	What makes the cents, not the dollar?	✔					
	Why is 99 not a dollar?		✔				
10:25	How would you write $200?	✔					
	What does 00 mean?	✔					
	Is that where Desmond saw a decimal point?	✔					
	What instrument ... temperature?	✔					
	How many kinds of therm? Name 2.	✔					
10:30	What is she looking for?	✔					
	What is a normal temperature?	✔					
	Have you seen your temperature written?	✔					
	Why do you think you need to use a decimal point?		✔				

Suggested Post-Observation Conference Strategies

To promote engagement in the post-observation conference, Mr. Taylor brought the form to the conference with only the verbatim questions listed. Mr. Taylor encouraged Mrs. Stevens to

- ♦ identify the level of thinking for each question noted and then to place a check mark in the grid (e.g., knowledge, comprehension, application, synthesis, evaluation);

- ♦ tally the number of questions at each level; and

- ♦ rework a few lower-order questions into a higher-order level.

Throughout the last step, Mr. Taylor asked probing questions: "What did you eventually want students to be able to do with the information being taught?" "How did the examples presented along with the questions help students understand the materials?" "Are there any clusters of questions that could have been extended beyond the Knowledge level?"

Mr. Taylor relied on the data to lead the discussion. He let Mrs. Stevens analyze the data, reflect on what the data meant for student learning, and rework questions that she had asked. Viewed within the framework of Bloom's Taxonomy, these questions allowed Mrs. Stevens to reconstruct her instruction in terms of her focus—levels of questions.

During the last 20 minutes of the post-observation conference, Mr. Taylor and Mrs. Stevens targeted a few strategies to try before the next classroom observation. Of the ideas discussed, Mrs. Stevens chose two:

- ♦ Have a colleague videotape a lesson that includes a question-and-answer segment. Watching the video, record the questions she asked. Analyze the cognitive level of student responses and identify any patterns in what she asked of her students.

- ♦ Use a professional release day to observe a teaching colleague at another school in the district.

Tool 2: Focus on Wait Time

This data collection tool helps teachers examine how long they wait before calling on students to answer their questions. Peggy Stanford, a ninth-grade English teacher, is seeking feedback on her use of wait time. During the pre-observation conference, Ms. Stanford told her assistant principal, Glenda Brown, that she feels her students are "just not with her," following the flow of book discussions.

Observation Focus

Ms. Stanford and Ms. Brown agree that the classroom observation will focus on wait time.

Observation Tool

Ms. Brown explains to Ms. Stanford that she will use a narrow-lens tool (Figure 6.9) to observe how long Ms. Stanford waits after asking a question before she calls on a student for a response.

Directions

Write just the stem of each question the teacher asks. Using a watch with a second hand, measure the elapsed time from the end of the question to the call for a response.

Figure 6.9. Wait Time

Date: 09/23/03   Beginning Time: 8:15   Ending Time: 9:05
Teacher: Peggy Stanford   Observer: Glenda Brown
Lesson Topic: *Rumble Fish*   Grade/Level: Grade 9, Honors English
Date of Post-observation Conference: 09/24/03

Teacher Question	Wait Time (in seconds)
…in what year?…James?	2
When you think of the lessons the characters learned by the end of the book, who do you think grew up the most?	3
How does the Siamese Fighting Fish come to be symbolic of the characters in this book?	5

Source: Adapted from Zepeda & Mayers (2000). Used with permission.

Suggested Post-Observation Conference Strategies

Ms. Brown prepared for the post-observation conference by thinking about the wait time in relation to the type of questions Ms. Stanford asked. During the post-observation conference, Ms. Brown

♦ invited Ms. Stanford to review her questions and the amount of wait time she allowed;

♦ suggested that Ms. Stanford analyze wait time in terms of the type of question asked, using Bloom's Taxonomy (Ms. Brown had added an extra column to the observation form; see I Figure 6.10); and

♦ encouraged Ms. Stanford to determine if there were any other patterns to questions—more or less wait time during question groupings (e.g., Evaluation vs. Knowledge).

Figure 6.10. Wait Time with Question Domain

Teacher Question	Wait Time (in seconds)	Question Domain
...in what year?...James?	2	Knowledge
When you think of the lessons the characters learned by the end of the book, who do you think grew up the most?	3	Synthesis, Evaluation
How does the Siamese Fighting Fish come to be symbolic of the characters in this book?	5	Evaluation
Is there any deeper meaning to letting the fish out of their tanks at the end of the story?	3	Evaluation

Tool 3: Focus on Cause-and-Effect Data

This tool gives the teacher information about the influence of the teacher's actions on student responses. This tool can be useful in observing a teacher's classroom management, questioning strategies, direction giving, and other teacher behaviors that ask for a student response. Nick Roberts, second-year science teacher at Altoon High School, is curious about why he often feels his students are "not following the program" during class periods, especially during labs where students have occasion to be out of their seats. Nick tells the science department chair, Frank Kempler, that at times he feels as if he is losing control of the learning environment.

Observation Focus

Nick Roberts and Frank Kempler agree that the classroom observation lens should be a narrow one. They decide on an interrelated focus: what Nick says or does and what students do in response.

Observation Tool

Frank Kempler explains that he will use a narrow lens to focus on what Nick says and does and its effect on what students say and do.

Directions

Divide a blank sheet of paper into two columns, as in Figure 6.11. Record teacher actions or words in the left-hand column. Record student response to these actions or words in the right-hand column.

Suggested Post-Observation Conference Strategies

Leaving the room, Frank Kempler passes the principal, who is responding to the call for assistance. Kempler is tempted to report to the principal what he just observed, but he decides to wait until after the post-observation conference with Nick. Frank decides to

- Ask Nick how he thought the lesson went.

- Ask Nick about his classroom procedures: What procedures and consequences are in place for students who do not come to class with their books? Does he have any extra books he could lend? What is his first line of defense when a student is off task?

- Encourage Nick to revisit his classroom procedures.

- Arrange for a follow-up observation during the same class period in two weeks.

- Encourage Nick to consult the principal about how to handle situations that escalate beyond what the teacher should deal with during a class period.

Figure 6.11. Teacher Action and Student Response

Date: 11/12/03   Beginning Time: 1:15   Ending Time: 2:30
Teacher: Nick Roberts   Observer: Frank Kempler
Lesson Topic: *Rumble Fish*   Grade/Level: Grade 9, Honors English
Date of Post-Observation Conference: 11/13/03

Teacher	Student Response and/or Activity
Bell (1:15)	Milling around room
Takes roll Makes announcements Collects homework	Quietly talking
Turns on overhead and says: "Take out your notebooks and open your book to page 140."	Students pull out materials. Red shirt slapping boy next to him (Blue shirt).
"Folks, heads up to the overhead and focus on the chapter objectives." Begins stating the objectives for the chapter.	Shuffling to get their books out and open to page 140. Seven students (out of 16) do not have books.
"Read from pages 140 to 145." Teacher sitting at desk reading a student essay.	Students without books: 2 are talking with each other 2 are sleeping 3 are reading from nearby student's books
"Who would like to offer a summary?"	4 students are still reading; 3 students (who did not have book) are talking with their neighbors; 2 students sleeping; 4 students raise their hands; 1 student asks a question out loud, "How can you expect us to finish reading 5 pages in 10 minutes," and another student blurts, "bite me."
"James, repeat what you said."	James: "Bite me."
"James, I just cannot believe you said, 'bite me.' Are you talking to me?"	Yeah, yeah, just "get bit," Roberts.
Pushes the call button for assistance.	8 students talking; 3 laughing; James walks to the door.

A Case Study

The principal, Joel Moody, asks Frank Kempler to write a detailed account of what occurred in Nick Robert's classroom. Moody then asks for detailed summaries of all classroom observations of Roberts.

♦ What issues are at stake here?

How should Kempler proceed with the request and his work with Roberts?

Tool 4: Focus on Variety of Instructional Methods

Regardless of the subject area, the grade level, or the teacher's experience, a single class period should include a variety of instructional methods. (The attention span of the average seventh-grade student is estimated at approximately 10 minutes; that of a ninth-grade student, 12 minutes.) Supervisors are encouraged to read books that detail the developmental levels typical of the students served at their site.

Karla Jones is starting a unit on young adult literature and the book *Rumble Fish* in her eighth-grade English class. Mrs. Jones wants feedback on the variety of instructional strategies she uses during a class period. On the one hand, she wants to prepare her students for the longer classes they will encounter in high school. On the other hand, she is concerned that extended lectures would lose students, given the developmental level of eighth-grade students.

Observation Focus

Mrs. Jones and her supervisor, principal Rita McCan, agree that the essential first step is to get baseline data on what instructional strategies Mrs. Jones uses during a typical class period. They further agree that other information could be useful: the length of each strategy, student engagement, and transitions from one activity to another. Recognizing that Mrs. Jones has 10 years of experience teaching at this level, Mrs. McCan believes that Mrs. Jones is capable of handling a variety of information; however, they both ask, "How much is too much?"

Observation Tool

Mrs. McCan explains to Mrs. Jones that she will use a narrow-lens tool to focus on the number of instructional strategies used, the length of each, and the activities students engage in during each. (Note that an observer can collect a great deal of data even through a narrow lens.)

Directions

For each instructional strategy used, indicate the time and what the teacher and the students are doing (see Figure 6.12).

Figure 6.12. Variety of Instructional Methods

Date: 03/12/03   Beginning Time: 9:00   Ending Time: 10:10
Teacher: Karla Jones   Observer: Rita McCan
Lesson Topic: *Rumble Fish*   Grade/Level: English, Grade 8
Date of Post-Observation Conference: 03/13/03

Time	Instructional Method	Teacher Behavior	Student Activities
9:00–9:10	Organizing lecture	Lecture, directions for small group work, break students into small groups.	Listening, taking notes, asking questions.
9:11–9:35	Cooperative learning	Assist students to get into small groups, passing out materials. Monitoring student work.	Getting into groups, selecting roles (recorder, timer). Discussing the symbol, the Siamese Fighting Fish; finding citations from the text to support ideas; group recorder presenting citations from the text in support of ideas; reading citations offered by other groups.
9:36–9:48	Large group discussion	Leading students to citations offered by groups.	
9:49–9:59	Question and answer	Ask questions.	Responding to questions (looking up citations to back up ideas). Asking questions, begin homework assignment.
10:00–10:10	Closure	Assignment given.	

Source: Zepeda & Mayers 2000. Used with permission.

Suggested Post-Observation Conference Strategies

Later the same day, Mrs. McCan visited Mrs. Jones for a few minutes and asked her to review the completed instrument so she could analyze the data on her own. The next day, Mrs. McCan and Mrs. Jones met before school to discuss the classroom observation. Mrs. McCan began the conversation with the question, "What patterns do you see?" During the post-observation conference, Mrs. Jones reviewed the various instructional strategies used, the amount of time spent on each, what students were doing during each, and what learning objectives were being met. Upon reflection, Mrs. Jones decided that she would experiment in the future by allotting more time to the large-group discussion (12 minutes was not enough time for students to reflect) and decreasing the amount of cooperative learning time. She reflected aloud that she sensed that students had completed the tasks assigned in groups about 10 minutes before she concluded the activity.

Tool 5: Examining Teacher–Student Discussion with a Focus on How Student Comments Are Incorporated into the Lesson

Instruction of any kind can gain when the teacher incorporates student responses into the lesson. Incorporating student responses as part of a lecture increases student engagement, promotes student ownership in the activities of the class, and keeps students focused on learning objectives. Student responses also cue the teacher to what students know and what areas need reteaching. Max Johnson, an English teacher, and his peer coach, Julie Thompson, have undertaken an action research project to examine what they do with student responses during classroom discussions.

Observation Focus

Max and Julie agree that the classroom observation will focus on what Max does to incorporate student responses in his classroom discussions.

Observation Tool

Julie will use a sheet of paper with four columns to record the time of the comment, Max's question or comment, the student's comments, and what Max does with student comments (Figure 6.13).

Directions

See above.

Figure 6.13. Incorporating Student
Comments and Ideas into Discussion

Date: 09/29/02   Beginning Time: 8:50   Ending Time: 9:30
Teacher: Max Johnson   Observer: Julie Thompson
Lesson Topic: *Rumble Fish*   Grade/Level: Grade 9, English I
Date of Post-Observation Conference: 09/29/02 (release period)

Time	Teacher question/ comment	Student comment	What the teacher does with the student comments
8:50	A symbol is an object that represents something else. What are the symbols in *Rumble Fish?*	SR1: Siamese rumble fish	Can you expand on this? (Max asks)
		SR2: The gangs are made up of people who can't get along with one another.	Cite an example of this from the text?
		SR3: See page 47.	Relate this to the end of the book.
		SR4: at the end, the Siamese fighting fish are let go.	Does this parallel the death of the character?

Source: Zepeda & Mayers, 2000. Used with permission.

Suggested Post-Observation Conference Strategies

Have the teacher track the type of responses students give and what the teacher does to incorporate student responses into the discussion. Track what strategies the teacher uses while incorporating comments (have students expand on each other's ideas, look up information in the book to support answers, have students write their ideas in notebooks, and so on).

Tool 6: Selective Verbatim—Teacher Verbal and Student Physical or Verbal Behaviors

This tool selectively records the exact words of the teacher, the students, or both. This tool can provide useful information about how the teacher asks questions, gives directions, praises or corrects students, and the like.

Sam Jilnick, a middle school math teacher, is having difficulties with his sixth-grade group of "slow" students. He believes that he is constantly issuing verbal corrections. Sam asks the lead teacher, Marty Burton, to observe him working with this group of students and to track the type and frequency of his verbal corrections.

Observation Focus

Marty will use the narrow tool of selective verbatim to capture the verbal corrections that Sam makes to his students and then record the student's reactions to the corrective statements.

Observation Tool

A sheet of paper with two columns, headed Teacher Verbal and Student Physical or Verbal Response.

Directions

Record the teacher's words in the left-hand column and student responses (verbal or physical) to these words in the right-hand column (see Figure 6.14).

Suggested Post-Observation Conference Strategies

Marty Burton leaves the classroom very concerned about the combative verbal exchanges she has just heard. She knows that the intensity of the encounter left the student and Sam at an impasse. Marty, as the lead teacher, takes responsibility for providing teachers the support they need. During the post-observation conference, Marty

- Asks Sam Jilnick to pinpoint where this confrontation really started.

- Creates a role-playing exercise. She plays Sam, and Sam plays the student. As Sam, she gives the student a pen and says, "I'll come back to you in a few minutes," then asks another student to share his work.

- Asks Sam to discuss how he can defuse negative verbal exchanges.

- Asks Sam what consequences he has used with this student in the past, what kind of relationship he has with this student, and whether he has spoken with the parents, guidance counselor, or other teachers about the student.

- Suggests that Sam read some materials she will provide on more proactive ways of dealing with student outbursts.

Figure 6.14. Teacher Verbal and Student Physical or Verbal Response

Date: 12/15/03   Beginning Time: 2:15   Ending Time: 2:45
Teacher: Sam Jilnick   Observer: Marty Burton
Lesson Topic: Verbs   Grade/Level: Grade 6
Date of Post-Observation Conference: 12/16/03 (prep period)

	Teacher verbal		Student physical or verbal response
1	Look at the Word of the Day on the board and write a sentence using the word.	1	Just one sentence or two?
2	One sentence, like we do every day.	2	We didn't do a word yesterday.
3	O.K. then like the one we did a few days ago.	3	
4	Tom, read your sentence.	4	I'm not done …I came in late.
5	Randy, let's hear your sentence.	5	My pen is out of ink … I can say the sentence I would have written.
6	Randy, this is the third time this week you have not come to class prepared to work.	6	Yeah, yeah, yeah. I only have pencils.
7	That's right… you can only use a pen to write class notes.	7	I don't like pens … you can't erase the marks.
8	Pens are what you must use… What don't you understand about this?	8	Why can't I use a pencil … Mrs. Scott lets us use pencils … so do all my teachers, but you.
9	That's right, young man, stand out in the hall for the next 15 minutes. Go to the office…now.	9	Jerk …

Tool 7: Wide-angle: No Focus

Some teachers might want to get a general idea of how things are going in the classroom; others might not be able to decide on a focus. The wide-angle lens allows the supervisor to report generally what is occurring in the classroom. Bob Cooper, in his seventh year of teaching second grade at St. Anthony's Elementary School, is curious about his third period block. Bob is experimenting with incorporating games into his lesson design, and he wants some feedback, in a general sense, on how things are going. Sandy Adams, the principal, will observe his classroom while Bob is incorporating games within the lesson.

Observation Focus

None.

Observation Tool

Running notes with a timeline of activities.

Directions

Write out events of the classroom as they occur (see Figure 6.15).

Suggested Post-Observation Conference Strategies

Sandy plans to ask Bob to examine what students were doing during the game and then to go over how he used time throughout the period for students to work on independent work (workbook assignment). To encourage reflection, Sandy develops a series of open-ended questions:

- What do you suppose students learned through the game?
- What will you do to follow up tomorrow?
- How can you assess the value of the game as part of instruction?
- Do you plan to use other games?

Tool 8: Focus on Calling Patterns and Patterns of Interaction

Teachers often wonder about their calling patterns. They want to know whom they are calling on and how often, whether they call on everyone, and whether they favor any one group or area of the classroom. Susan Petrulis, a middle school social studies teacher, wonders whether she plays favorites. Susan is concerned because a parent complained to her that she was ignoring her daughter and a few other students who were recently suspended for smoking. More importantly, however, Susan just wants to know whether she is providing many opportunities for students to answer. Susan asked Francie Parker, the assistant principal, to observe her, focusing on her calling patterns.

Observation Focus

Calling and interaction patterns during a class period.

Figure 6.15. Running Notes on
Classroom Events with a Timeline

Date: 01/12/03   Beginning Time: 10:00   Ending Time: 11:00
Teacher: Bob Cooper   Observer: Sandy Adams
Lesson Topic: Fractions   Grade/Level: Grade 2
Date of Post-Observation Conference: 01/13/03 (after school)

Lecture (10 Minutes)	10:00	lesson begins with discussion back and forth between teacher/students
	10:05	lecture/discussion about fractions (how to reduce)
	10:10	instructions for game/game begins
Game (20 Minutes)	10:15	game continues: exploring fractions
	10:20	game continues: comparing fractions, using cards
	10:25	game continues
	10:30	game ends; math book and reporting sheet-work begins
Group Work (20 Minutes)	10:35	reviewing learning from lesson; connecting with previous learning
	10:40	work with problems in math book: lecture—explaining reducing a fraction
	10:45	work in book: working independently on assignment in math book(teacher helping individual students)
	10:50	continuing to work on assignment; independent work
	10:55	students working independently and in small groups on assignment
	11:00	teacher calls group back together; lesson ends—class goes to assembly

Observation Tool

Seating chart with legend of codes for calling and interaction patterns.

Directions

Identify with the teacher the most common calling patterns (entire class responding, individual response, individual assistance, and so on). Develop a code for each. During the observation, track calling patterns on seating chart (see Figure 6.16).

Suggested Post-Observation Conference Strategies

The data recorded on the chart allow the teacher to review her own calling patterns (frequency, gender, and so forth). As an alternative, the observer might record the data chronologically, yielding the portrait shown in Figure 6.17 (p. 154).

Francie Parker can then lead Susan to look beyond the number of times she calls on or gives assistance to individual students to see the bigger picture: What does her instruction and interaction look like? Does she spend too much time giving certain individuals attention, excluding other students?

Tool 9: Focus on Tracking Transition Patterns

Transitioning from one activity to another is an important part of instruction, especially for longer class periods (regardless of the grade or subject matter). Mary Barker, a ninth-grade English teacher, is new to teaching in the extended block schedule. She has asked her department chair, Frank Donaldson, to observe her during the first block period. She wants Frank to give her feedback about the transitions she uses.

Observeration Focus

Transitions between classroom activities; transitions from one instructional method to another.

Observeration Tool

Frank will use a form he designed to track transitions.

Directions

Record the instruction/activity, the transition, and the student response (see Figure 6.18, p. 155).

Suggested Post-Observation Conference Strategies

Encourage the teacher to examine the transitions and how students respond.

(Text continues on page 155.)

Figure 6.16. Tracking Calling Patterns

Date: 10/29/02   Beginning Time: 11:00   Ending Time: 11:55
Teacher: Susan Petrulis   Observer: Francie Parker
Lesson Topic: Social Studies   Grade/Level: Grade 7, Social Studies
Date of Post-Observation Conference: 10/30/02 (after school)

Legend: ECR—Entire Class Responding; R—Response;
           IH—Individual Help; Q—Question; C—Comment

Front of Room

	A	B	C	D
1.	**CHARLES** 11:30-R	**JAMES** 11:33-R 11:37-R 11:53-R	**MARY** (sitting in back) 11:30-R 11:46-Reading 11:47-R/R	**SAM** 11:04-R 11:12-Q 11:26-IH 11:51-R
2.	**CHRISTINE** 11:20-Q to teacher 11:31-R (w/repeat)	**TONY** 11:03-R 11:07-C (we're good!) 11:08-R 11:30-C 11:39-R 11:49-huh? To Randy 11:49-Reading 11:52-R	**ANDREA** 11:13-C made by teacher 11:23-IH 11:52-R	**RANDY** 11:03-R 11:48-Reading 11:51-R
3.	**MICHAEL** 11:04-R 11:52-R	**TIFFANY** 11:03-R 11:29-C 11:30-R 11:31-R/R 11:45-Q	**JEAN** 11:11-C/R 11:26-IH 11:33-R 11:43-C 11:53-R	**SANDY** 11:11-Q (moving) 11:51-R
4.	**PATRICK** Suspended	**JEFF**	**KRISTY** 11:06-Q 11:23-IH 11:28-R 11:32-R 11:33-R 11:47-R 11:50-Reading 11:52-R 11:53-R 11:53-R	**AMBER** 11:09-C 11:39-Q 11:48-Q
5.	**ANDREW** 11:04-R 11:47-Reading 11:51-R 11:53-R	**TYSON** 11:13-C made by teacher 11:29-C 11:32-R 11:36-R 11:43-Q 11:44-Q 11:51-R		**KATE** Absent

Figure 6.17. Tracking Chronologically

11:00	Start observation Sponge activity on board	11:06	ECR (Noise is back)	11:18	Comment to class on procedures after finishing	11:35	ECR
11:01	Door closed Check roll Students actively working	11:07	ECR–then gone	11:22	Announces 5 more minutes	11:36	A few comments from various people ECR
11:02	Question of day Start talking ECR Review	11:08	ECR	11:23	Working with Mary	11:37	Class responding Class responding
11:03	Review ECR	11:09	ECR	11:26	Announces 2 more minutes	11:38	Back to Barb
11:04	ECR (uses SRA technique)	11:10	Explaining events of class	11:27	Calls time	11:39	Comments
11:05	ECR Noise in background Ignoring	11:10	Procedures: books will be passed out	11:28	Announces to check vocabulary ECR	11:40	ECR
		11:11	Reminder of what books are for; monitoring class; students actively working; QUIET	11:29	ECR	11:45	Trade and grade
		11:16	Sitting at front *quiet* (still)	11:32	ECR General comments from class	11:46	ECR
				11:34	ECR (during experiment)	11:48	ECR
						11:51	ECR
						11:53	ECR
						11:54	ECR

Figure 6.18. Transition Tracking Chart

Date: 11/12/02   Beginning Time: 8:00   Ending Time: 9:00
Teacher: Mary Barker   Observer: Frank Donaldson
Lesson Topic: *Rumble Fish*   Grade/Level: Grade 9, English I
Date of Post-Observation Conference: 11/12/02 (4th block)

Number of Students Present: __27__		
Instruction/Activity	**Transition**	**Student Response**
8:00 Getting students into cooperative groups	Gives directions for small cooperative group. Stops movement to give clarifying instructions.	Students meander, finding their group members; 4 students ask clarifying questions during movement.
8:20 Getting students back into large group	Flicks lights on and off, asks Group 1 to send their rep to the front of the room to give a summary.	Students are moving desks, ripping paper from their notebooks.

Source: Zepeda & Mayers, 2000. Used with permission.

Tool 10: Focus on Tracking the Beginning and Ending (Closure) of Class

The start and the end of any given class are very important. The beginning of a class period sets the tone for all that follows. This is typically a busy time; students are moving around (entering the classroom, sharpening pencils, pulling out materials from their backpacks), and the teacher tends to housekeeping duties (taking attendance, making announcements) and gives directions for getting started ("Open books to page 20"). At the beginning of a class, effective teachers provide advance organizers that ready students for learning.

The ending of class brings closure to the events of the period and helps focus students on how to prepare for the next day. Often, teachers spend five to ten minutes recapping what was learned or what objectives were accomplished. This check for understanding and mastery informs the teacher's decisions about the next day's instruction.

The first and last segments of the instructional period can offer teachers important insights about other classroom events. Amy Kleibar, a first-year English teacher, is experiencing difficulties with beginning and ending her classes. She confides her concerns to Jan Fisher, the dean of students and a former English teacher, who offers to observe Amy.

Observation Focus

Although Jan will observe Amy's class for the entire period, she will collect data only at the beginning and ending of the seventh period.

Observation Tool

Jan will use a form she has developed.

Directions

Record what the teacher and students do at the beginning and ending of the period (see Figure 6.19, p. 157).

Suggested Post-Observation Conference Strategies

Jan Fischer feels conflicted. She knows exactly why Amy is having trouble beginning and ending her class—she lacks clear procedures at the beginning, and she is rushed and disorganized at the end. However, as dean of students she knows most of these students; they are "frequent flyers" in her office. Still, Jan wants Amy to work at developing and then implementing clear procedures for starting and ending class. Jan decides on the following course:

- Lead Amy through the data and ask her to reconstruct what the beginning and ending of class would look like if she had rules.

- Ask Amy to develop one or two rules for beginning class and one or two rules for ending class.

- Role-play implementation, so Amy can anticipate how students might respond to new rules and procedures.

- Arrange for Amy to visit a second-year teacher who had similar problems and was able to overcome the difficulties of establishing routines during the second month of school.

- Schedule two follow-up observations, one for the first 20 minutes of class and the second for the last 20 minutes.

Figure 6.19. Tracking Beginning and Ending Classroom Procedures

Date: 10/12/02   Beginning Time: 8:45   Ending Time: 9:30
Teacher: Amy Kleibar   Observer: Jan Fischer
Lesson Topic: NA   Grade/Level: Grade 9, English I
Date of Post-Observation Conference: 10/12/02 (prep period)

Beginning of the Period	Student Behavior	Ending of the Period	Student Behavior
8:45 to 8:50 Attendance taken as students enter the room. Teacher in the doorway stopping students as they enter to take off coats and hats.	Students entering the room and stopping by T's desk to pick up graded papers; students comparing grades as they walk to their desks. (Clusters of students clog the doorway and area around T's desk.)	9:24 Recap the symbols developed in the book.	Students pushing their chairs together; 5 students putting books and other class materials in book bags. Student raises hand: "Are we going to have a quiz tomorrow?" Another student: "Are our essays due next week?" Another: "When will we get more information about the essay?"
Bell rings at 8:50. T closes door and picks up papers left on desk—calls students up to the front of the room to pick up papers.	Students sitting at desk while T gives students their papers; student in row 3 trips a student; 2 students in row 5 push around books while walking up the aisles.		
Announcements from the activities office; opens the door for late students; stops at the computer station to log tardy students. Review due dates for next essay.	Students sitting at desk with 9 students turned around talking to other students; 5 students are digging materials out from their book bags; 3 students lined up at the pencil sharpener.	9:28 Bring notebooks tomorrow, and I'll add more information about the essay.	
9:05 Review my comments on your papers. Revisions are due tomorrow—rewrite only the parts of the essay circled in green.	3 students standing in a line in front of the pencil sharpener. 2 students crumple their essays and toss into garbage can.	9:29 Back to the symbols	
9:09 Directions: "Pull out notebooks and book."	5 students looking for books; 3 go to the bookshelf for a book; 5 students huddle with nearby students to share books.	9:30 Bell rings. T: Stay in your seats, we are not done.	Students begin to stand and leave.
9:12 Open-ended question: "Why is it fitting that the story ends in a pet store?"	Students ask if they are going to finish the group project from the previous day.	T reminds students to bring notebooks.	

Summary

The classroom observation requires preparation—conducting a pre-observation conference, selecting a data collection technique, and then readying for

the post-observation conference. Given the fast pace of events in a typical classroom, mastering the techniques of classroom observation takes time. The choice of instrument or technique (wide-angle or narrow-angle) depends on factors such as the focus, the teacher's experience level, and the supervisor's experience level. In any case, the goal is to collect data that will make sense for the teacher during the post-observation conference.

The success of the post-observation conference depends in part on the quality of the data collected during the classroom observation. Strategies and skills for the post-observation conference are discussed in the next chapter.

Suggested Reading

Acheson, K. A., & Gall, M. D. (1997). *Techniques in the clinical supervision of teachers: Preservice and inservice applications* (4th ed.). White Plains, NY: Longman.

Costa, A. L., & Garmston, R. J. (1994). *Cognitive coaching: A foundation for renaissance schools.* Norwood, MA: Christopher-Gordon.

Glatthorn. A. A. (1997). *Differentiated supervision* (2nd ed.). Alexandria, VA: Association for Supervision and Curriculum Development.

Glickman, C. D., Gordon, S. P., & Ross-Gordon, J. M. (1998). *Supervision of instruction: A developmental approach.* (4th ed.). Needham Heights, MA: Allyn and Bacon.

7

The Post-Observation Conference

Instructional Leaders Conduct Post-Observation Conferences after Formal Classroom Observations

In this Chapter ...

- ♦ The purposes of the post-observation conference
- ♦ Lesson reconstruction, constructivism, and the zone of proximal development
- ♦ Preparing for the post-observation conference
- ♦ Supervisory approaches and the post-observation conference
- ♦ Feedback, trust, and the Johari Window revisited
- ♦ After the post-observation conference, then what?

The primary intent of formative instructional supervision is to provide ongoing developmental opportunities for teachers to explore their teaching and student learning. The post-observation conference is the final stage in a cycle of clinical supervision, but the word *final* is deceptive, for the post-observation conference is a learning opportunity that spurs further growth. The post-observation conference is grounded in the reality of the teacher's world—the classroom, where learning occurs for both students and teachers. At its core, the post-observation conference presents a forum where teacher and supervisor talk about the events of the classroom observation.

159

Like children, adults are active learners. Teachers learn by examining data that reflect their classroom practices. If appropriately and accurately presented in the post-observation conference, these data can help teachers see and hear their practices and the effect of these practices on student learning. Adults need to be able to construct meaning by reconstructing the events of the classroom; the data collected in the classroom observation provide the building blocks for teachers to assemble and reassemble knowledge with the assistance of the supervisor or a peer.

The supervisor's communication skills and the trust between the teacher and supervisor can enhance the presentation of data and may motivate teachers to examine their practices more closely during future cycles of supervision.

The Purposes of the Post-Observation Conference

The post-observation conference provides opportunities for teachers to talk about, inquire into, and reflect on their practices with the assistance of the supervisor (or, in the case of peer coaching, a teaching colleague). The purposes and intents of the post-observation conference are for the teacher and supervisor collaboratively to

- ◆ review and analyze the data collected in terms of the focus they established in the pre-observation conference;

- ◆ develop a working plan for ongoing growth and development, predicated on what is observed in the classroom and what is discussed in the post-observation conference; and

- ◆ ready the teacher to set a focus in the next pre-observation conference.

In the post-observation conference, the teacher does not listen passively as the supervisor reads from notes; rather, the teacher reconstructs the events of the classroom with the supervisor or peer as facilitator.

Lesson Reconstruction, Constructivism, and the Zone of Proximal Development

Lesson Reconstruction

Bellon and Bellon (1982) promoted a post-observation conference technique called *lesson reconstruction,* in which the teacher reconstructs the events of the lesson based solely on the data derived from the classroom observation. Lesson reconstruction puts learning from the data at center stage, with teachers engaged as active learners. Lesson reconstruction is constructivist, in that "learners construct meaning from what they experience; thus, learning is an active meaning-making process" (Glatthorn, 1990, p. 6).

Constructivism

As active learners, teachers need to construct their own meanings based on what they do and experience. During the post-observation conference, supervisors can support the construction of knowledge by fostering critical inquiry and reflection on practice so that knowledge and insights about teaching can be

- physically constructed by learners who are involved in their environment;

- symbolically constructed by learners who are making their own representations of action;

- socially constructed by learners who convey their meaning making to others; and

- theoretically constructed by learners who try to explain things they do not understand (Gagnon & Collay, 2001).

The Zone of Proximal Development

Another concept that enriches the supervisor's approach to the post-observation conference is the *zone of proximal development* (Vygotsky, 1978). Vygotsky asserts that the learner individually constructs knowledge with the assistance of another person who can help the learner rise to higher levels of knowledge or practice. Working in the zone of proximal development, the learner keeps stretching to construct new knowledge slightly above his current level of knowing. Figure 7.1 depicts the zone of proximal development as described by Vygotsky.

Figure 7.1. The Zone of Proximal Development

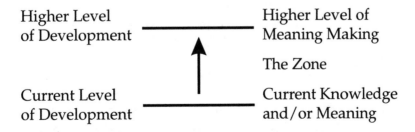

The key tenet of constructivist theory as it relates to supervision "is that people learn by actively constructing knowledge, weighing new information against their previous understanding, thinking about and working through discrepancies (on their own and with others), and coming to a new understanding" (O'Neil, 1998 p. 51).

Lyons and Pinnell (2001) offer eight generalized principles for organizing and implementing constructivist-based learning for adults. These principles (see Figure 7.2) can illustrate what effective supervisors do in the post-observation conference to encourage growth and development.

Figure 7.2. Organizing and Developing a Constructivist-Based Learning Environment for Adults

Principles of Constructivist-Based
Learning Activities for Adults

♦ Principle 1:   Encourage active participation.

♦ Principle 2:   Organize small-group discussion around common concerns.

♦ Principle 3:   Introduce new concepts in context.

♦ Principle 4:   Create a safe environment.

♦ Principle 5:   Develop participants' conceptual knowledge through conversations around shared experience.

♦ Principle 6:   Provide opportunities for participants to use what they know to construct knowledge.

♦ Principle 7:   Look for shifts in teachers' understanding over time.

♦ Principle 8:   Provide additional experiences for participants who have not yet developed [the] needed conceptual understanding[s].

Source: Lyons & Pinnell, 2001, pp. 4–6.

The principles of constructivism, when applied to the post-observation conference, can help teachers make better sense of observation data so that "the focus is puzzling, inquiring and problem solving" (Sergiovanni & Starratt, 1998, pp. 266–267).

Preparing for the
Post-Observation Conference

Meeting the professional needs of teachers as adult learners is a time-consuming endeavor for the instructional supervisor. Heavily involved in non-instructional tasks, supervisors often are distanced from classroom environments. The longer supervisors hold positions that separate them from regular contact with students and teachers, the more noticeable this distance becomes to teachers.

Effective post-observation conferences

♦ occur within 48 hours of the observation;

♦ are held in the classroom where the observation occurred;

♦ invite ongoing dialogue between the teacher and supervisor.

Time is important; if too much time elapses between the observation and the conference, the classroom data lose meaning and teachers lose motivation to work with them. Place is significant; holding the conference in the principal's office puts the principal in a position of authority, while the classroom offers the context of the learning environment to enrich the discussion. Atmosphere is essential; the post-observation conference opens the door to future dialogue and growth.

Effective supervisors take time to prepare for the post-observation conference. In the original models of clinical supervision, both Cogan (1973) and Goldhammer (1969) included a planning stage in which the supervisor assembled and interpreted data before meeting with the teacher. This planning time gives the supervisor the opportunity to organize the raw data gathered during the observation. Teaching is fast-paced, and the supervisor is recording observations at an equally fast pace, not always with perfect clarity. In its final form, the data must be clear and understandable to both the teacher and the supervisor. To lay the groundwork for a successful post-observation conference, the supervisor tackles several tasks:

Revisit the Focus (Purpose) of the Classroom Observation

Reviewing the data, the supervisor looks for direct or striking examples of classroom practices that relate specifically to the focus. One approach is to identify events that contributed to achieving an objective or prevented the teacher from achieving an objective. In addition to revisiting the focus, the principal might refer to Figure 4.7 (pp. 105-106) to get a sense of the Criteria for Talking about Teaching.

Resist the Temptation to Infuse Personal Values and Beliefs

Effective supervisors avoid preconceived judgments. Supervision is ongoing and formative. Acheson and Gall (1997) believe it is the supervisor's job to hold up the "mirror of practice" for the teacher. The biases or values of the supervisor cloud the mirror and get in the way of teachers as they work to make sense of their practice.

Determine Whether Observation Notes Need to be Rewritten

Rewriting does not mean adding new data or the supervisor's own ideas. More often, it means filtering out extraneous data. New supervisors, in their eagerness to do a good job at collecting data, will record every word or incident—even those unrelated to the observation focus. These can obscure the notes related directly to the focus, and depending on the experience level of the teacher, can lead to information overload.

Develop a Strategy for Presenting the Data Collected During the Observation

Providing the teacher with objective feedback means not only displaying the data clearly but also continually returning to the data for clarification, explanation, or extension during the post-observation conference. The observer's role is to facilitate the teacher's self-analysis and reflection, based on the data. The conference plan should keep the teacher reflecting and analyzing the events of the classroom.

Frame an Opening to Get the Teacher Thinking and Talking about Teaching

Effective invitations to dialogue, also called icebreakers, are open-ended statements related to some aspect of teaching. Figure 7.3 presents examples of icebreakers for the post-observation conference.

Embrace the Spontaneity of the Discussion

Although effective post-observation conferences are planned around the focus, spontaneous interaction makes clear that the supervisor is willing to listen and able to acknowledge the teacher's point of view regarding the self-assessment of strengths and weaknesses.

Figure 7.3. Sample Post-Observation
Icebreaker Statements

Icebreaker Statements	*Conversation Stoppers*
Think back to [some aspect of the lesson or the class] and tell me about it.	Prove to me that the students were prepared for independent practice.
The approach you chose to break students into small groups helped students learn how to cooperate. Tell me how you were able to get students to this level of cooperation.	No matter what you say, I just can't believe that the students will be ready to work in cooperative groups.
Tell me more about [some aspect of the class, student response, an instructional method, predictions about how students will perform on an assessment].	I'd like for you to turn in the results of your next quiz. I saw too many students struggling with their work during independent practice. Don't you think that more guided practice would have been more appropriate?
When you looked at Johnny, he knew immediately to stop talking.	Don't get too confident about Johnny, he'll talk while you are working with other students.
After the small group activity began, you used the down time to help students who had been absent the day before	Just analyze my notes and then get back to me if you have any questions about my assessment of your teaching.
How did you know that the student would try to…	Stop babying these kids; trust me, I know them better than you do.

Supervisory Approaches and
the Post-Observation Conference

To conduct a positive post-observation conference, the supervisor must have a facilitative style—open to hearing what the teacher has to say. The teacher's point of view must permeate the discussion. Talking about teaching is a cooperative endeavor. It is the supervisor's responsibility to engage the teacher in reviewing, analyzing, and reflecting on data. The post-observation conference is the forum for supervisors to help teachers make meaning of their practices. Through effort, patience, and willingness to be of assistance, supervisors can help teachers move up a notch in their development. The goal is for supervisors to understand the learning needs of their teachers and for supervisors and teachers to chart the next steps in the learning process.

To establish a cooperative learning experience for the teacher, the supervisor's style and approach to communication must promote teacher talk. Figure 7.4 identifies supervisory approaches for promoting teacher talk, inquiry, and reflection.

Feedback, Trust, and the Johari Window Revisited

Feedback

Kallick (1997) believes that "learners are in a state of continuously working to improve, grow, and learn" (p. 216), and one strategy to promote learning is to receive feedback on performance. For best results, the supervisor uses the data collected in the observation to frame feedback. Feedback, in a sense, is "the breakfast of champions"—teachers need and want to know how they are doing and what they can do to improve or modify an approach.

Feedback can be constructive or destructive. Consider these two statements.

Statement 1: "Mrs. Ritter, you really need to take the workshop. All the questions you asked were lower-level ones. Students were obviously bored with your inability to ask for more than recall of information."

Statement 2: "Mrs. Ritter, your insight about your questions asking students for recall reminds me of how I used to ask opening questions. I benefited from the county workshop, *Questioning Strategies That Promote Higher-Order Thinking.* This session is on the schedule for next month; would you be interested in attending? We have the funds and with advance notice, I can lock in a sub for you."

Statement 1 is destructive; it is too blunt, and it puts down the teacher with a personal attack. Statement 2 communicates the same message—the teacher needs assistance with questioning strategies—but in a more proactive way.

Proactive feedback provides objective insight based on data without criticizing the teacher or finding fault. It encourages risk-taking and promotes changes in practice. Destructive feedback, by contrast, attacks aspects that are beyond control (such as the sound of the teacher's voice), or belittles teachers by compiling data that point only to weaknesses. Figure 7.5 (p. 168) lists characteristics of effective feedback.

(Text continues on page 168.)

Figure 7.4. Supervisory Approaches for
Promoting Teacher Talk, Inquiry, and Reflection

Supervisory Approach	*Example*
Remain objective by providing the teacher with observational data that is value-free and nonjudgmental.	Here are the events that led to the small group…
Listen more—talk less—in order to hear (understand) what the teacher is trying to communicate.	Examining the following notes, tell me what responses you anticipated from students after you asked for…
Acknowledge, paraphrase, and ask probing/clarifying questions that encourage the teacher to talk more. Open-ended questions help the teacher make discoveries, identify recurring patterns, and reflect on possible alternatives or extensions to instructional practices.	From your point of view, what made this lesson successful?
Encourage the teacher to expand on statements that share beliefs about teaching, learning, and students.	When the student in the red shirt, said: "This is stupid," what made it possible for you to continue with the activity?
State what went well and ask reflective questions to focus on what needs improvement from the teacher's point of view.	The small group activity really worked well. How do you think the transition back to large group could have been different?
Avoid giving directive types of advice—even if asked. Instead, engage the teacher in role-playing reprises of events you observed, then invite extended thinking. Role-playing and simulations that reflect the teacher's practices are more realistic. (This is one reason the post-observation conference should take place in the teacher's classroom; this extends the realism needed to make credible decisions for future improvement.)	Let me pretend I am a student in your fourth hour class. How would you help me?
Refuse to engage in talk not related to what you directly observed or to the improvement of instruction.	That thought is important. After the post-observation conference, I'll share your idea with the dean of students.
Offer to return for further observations in order to keep the momentum going for the teacher.	When would be a good time for me to come back to see the students apply the formula?
Provide ongoing support for the decisions the teacher makes in the post-observation conference by investigating with the teacher follow-up learning or enrichment activities.	The district is offering an after-school workshop on higher order thinking. Perhaps you'd like to go…Mrs. Simpson signed up for the workshop. I'll call in a reservation for you.
Be aware of nonverbal behavior that can send mixed messages.	Looking at the clock, facial expressions, body language such as folded arms.

Figure 7.5. Characteristics of Effective Feedback

Effective feedback in the post-observation conference:

♦ Supports the teacher in examining both the positive and the not-so-positive aspects of practice.

♦ Promotes footholds for follow-up.

♦ Nurtures a sense of worth and positive self-esteem.

♦ Facilitates self-assessment and self-discovery.

♦ Focuses on a few key areas.

♦ Describes accurately what was observed.

♦ Is authentic and free of meaningless or patronizing platitudes.

♦ Clarifies and expands ideas for both the teacher and the observer.

♦ Deals with the concrete examples observed (actions, behaviors, words of the teacher or students).

♦ Promotes goal setting and the development of strategies.

♦ Avoids
  • making assumptions about teachers;
  • overloading the teacher with detail after detail after detail;
  • evaluating the teacher's overall credibility as a teacher;
  • asserting or making inferences about the teacher; and
  • judging and labeling a practice as good or bad.

♦ Guides the teacher to think beyond the lesson observed.

♦ Accepts and incorporates the points the teacher makes as part of the feedback process.

In an attempt to be helpful, some supervisors fall into the trap of overwhelming the teacher with too much information. Beginning supervisors, in particular, may seek to establish their credibility by offering a laundry list of observations based on their view of the lesson. But supervision is not about the supervisor; supervision is about the teacher and the learning opportunity that data and feedback from an observation can provide.

The tenor of the feedback in the post-observation conference sets the tone for future interaction between the supervisor and teacher. However, even carefully framed feedback may not be well received. The way a teacher receives feedback depends on variables such as the degree of trust between the supervisor and teacher, the experience level of the teacher, the patterns of communication at the school, and the conditions surrounding the classroom observation.

Trust

Supervisors who are new to the setting or who are implementing new supervisory practices need to establish their credibility. New supervisors do not have a personal history; as unknown commodities, they must first establish a foundation for their supervisory relationships with teachers. Trust, built over time and established by the supervisor's words and deeds, is the cornerstone of the supervisory relationship.

Poor communication can compromise trust. Supervisors are wise to be aware of the trust-blocking responses outlined by Pascarelli and Ponticell (1994), presented in Figure 7.6 (p. 170). What is said and how can enhance or impede future interactions between a teacher and supervisor.

Effective communication underpins the collaboration of supervisor and teacher in the pre-and post-observation conferences.

The Johari Window Revisited

The principles of the Johari Window were introduced in Chapter 5 in relation to communication during the pre-observation conference. (See Figure 5.4 for a portrayal of the Johari Window.) To recap: The four panes of the Johari Window are the open pane (aspects known to the self and to others), the hidden pane (known to the self, unknown to others), the blind pane (unknown to the self, known to others), and the unknown pane (unknown to the self and to others).

During the post-observation conference, the supervisor leads the teacher in exploring aspects of his teaching or other classroom behaviors. The flavor and intensity of this learning opportunity will vary depending on the teacher's awareness of these aspects at the start. Exploration in the open pane is relatively straightforward; exploration of aspects the teacher has kept in the hidden pane requires a deeper foundation of trust. Through objective feedback, the supervisor can help the teacher open the blind pane and become aware of behaviors as others see them. Through listening and support, the supervisor can help the teacher explore the unknown pane, learning about possible areas of weakness—but also resources and strengths—that neither has recognized until now.

Figure 7.6. Trust-Blocking Responses

- **Evaluating**   Phrases such as the following tend to evoke defensiveness: "You should ...," "Your responsibility here is ...," "You are wrong about ..."

- **Advice-giving**   Advice is best given if requested; responses such as "Why don't you just ...," "You would be better off ...," or "Your best action is ..." can go in one ear and out the other if unsolicited.

- **Topping**   "That's nothing, you should have seen ...," "Well, in my class ...," "When that happened to me...," "You think you have it bad, well..." are phrases of one-upm anship. They shift attention from the person who wants to be listened to and leaves him/her feeling unimportant.

- **Diagnosing**   Phrases that tell others what they feel ("What you need is ...," "The reason you feel that way is ...," "You really don't mean that ...," "Your problem is ...") can be a two-edged sword, leaving the person feeling pressured (if the speaker is wrong) or feeling exposed or caught (if the speaker is right).

- **Warning**   "You had better ...," "If you don't ...," "You have to ...," or "You must ..." can produce resentment, resistance, or rebellion if the recipient feels the finger of blame pointed in his/her direction.

- **Lecturing**   "Don't you realize ...," "Here is where you are wrong ...," "The facts simply prove ...," or "Yes, but ...," can make the person feel inferior or defensive. Full, descriptive data and problem-solving questioning allow the individual to make logical decisions for him or herself.

- **Devaluating**   "It's not so bad ...," "Don't worry ...," "You'll get over it ...," or "Oh, you really don't feel that way ..." take away or deny the feelings of the speaker. Conveying nonacceptance of the speaker's feelings creates a lack of trust, feelings of inferiority or fault, and fear of risk-taking.

Source: Pascarelli & Ponticell, 1994.

After the Post-Observation Conference, Then What?

The end is the beginning. The post-observation conference can serve to link supervision to staff development and evaluation. In Chapter 3, Figure 3.2 (p. 61) portrays a visual for linking supervision, staff development, and evaluation. Through completing a full cycle of clinical supervision, both the teacher and the supervisor are aware of areas to focus through staff development that could include such activities as

- attending workshops, seminars, and conferences;
- observing another teacher in the building or district;
- enrolling in a graduate course;
- engaging in action research with a common grade or subject area teacher;
- reading a book or a series of articles related to a topic of interest; and
- developing or refining a portfolio.

The possibilities for staff development are endless, and staff development should relate directly to helping teachers capitalize on the information learned from the processes of supervision—the pre-observation conference, data collected in an extended classroom observation, and the insights gained from examining, reflecting, and inquiring on these data in the post-observation conference. The ultimate goal of efforts between the teacher and principal is to promote student learning.

Many school systems assist teachers through the development of a plan. A professional growth plan would include goals, areas for the teacher to explore, and ways in which the teacher can explore these areas. At the end of the post-observation conference, the teacher and supervisor map activities included in Figure 7.7 (p. 172).

Figure 7.7 should be adapted for the context in which supervision occurs. The point is effective supervision does not end once the post-observation conference has concluded; effective supervisors seek ways to keep the momentum for learning from once cycle of supervision to the next.

Summary

The post-observation conference holds great promise as a supervisory tool. During this time, teachers have the opportunity to analyze and make sense of data that bring into focus some aspect of their teaching. Lesson reconstruction as advocated by Bellon and Bellon (1982) engages the teacher in reconstructing

Figure 7.7. Professional Growth Plan

Date: 11/12/02   Teacher: Anne Hawkins
Grade/Level: Freshmen English

1. Highlights from the post-observation conference:

2. Area(s) to target:

3. Short-term goal:

4. Resources needed:

5. Follow-up:

6. Date to begin the next cycle of supervision:

the events of the classroom using data to analyze effectiveness. The supervisor's objective feedback positions the teacher to make informed judgments about practice and to develop further plans for growth and change.

Suggested Reading

Acheson, K. A., & Gall, M. D. (1997). *Techniques in the clinical supervision of teachers: Preservice and inservice applications* (4th ed.). White Plains, NY: Longman.

Bellon, J. J., & Bellon, E. C. (1982). *Classroom supervision and instructional improvement: A synergetic process* (2nd ed.). Dubuque, IA: Kendall/Hunt.

Bryk, A. S., & Schneider, B. (2002). *Trust in schools: A core resource for improvement.* New York: Russell Sage.

Calabrese, R. L., & Zepeda, S. J. (1997). *The reflective supervisor.* Larchmont, NY: Eye on Education.

8

No Principal Needs to Stand Alone

The message of this book is a simple one—principals need to exert their instructional leadership to assist teachers further develop as professionals while meeting the needs of students. No other activity can take priority over instructional leadership.

The classroom is the heart of the school, and this is where the principal as instructional leader needs to focus time and energy. However, the principal does not need to stand alone to support the professional development of teachers. Although there are differences in the composition of administrative and supervisory personnel across schools, most administrative teams include assistant principals. High schools include the leadership of department chairs; many middle schools include the leadership of lead teachers; and elementary schools include the leadership of instructional coordinators. Depending on the school's size and location (e.g., urban, suburban, or rural), additional positions such as an associate principal or an instructional dean might round out the administrative team. The people who fill these positions have varying involvement with the instructional program.

It falls to the principal to examine the pool of supervisory personnel and to work at building new instructional leadership roles with these professionals. By developing an instructional leadership team, the principal is in a solid position to multiply efforts to assist teachers.

The type of instructional leadership explored in this book will thrive by including the members of the administrative team. Modeling and mentoring are powerful teaching tools, and the principal's efforts to promote instructional leadership skills in others will yield untold results within the school. Considering that most assistant principals aspire to the principalship, then, in turn, these individuals will work with their administrative team using what was modeled as a template for instructional leadership. The principal who mentors members of the administrative team creates a legacy of instructional leaders.

Members of the administrative team, like the principal, need to examine their beliefs and practices regarding professional development. Without such an examination, the school's administrative team will not be synchronized to work alongside the principal and others to meet the needs of teachers as they work at improving instructional practices. The administrative team needs to learn how to work together to

♦ build a unified vision for supervision and professional development;

♦ create a healthy culture;

♦ serve as valuable resources to teachers to meet their needs;

♦ coordinate and provide appropriate learning opportunities based on these needs; and

♦ grow as professionals from their work in the school.

Effective principals cast the net to include others in the work of instructional leadership. With the involvement of administrative team members working under the same set of assumptions and values about teachers and their growth, there can be a more powerful message sent to teachers—support for their efforts at becoming better teachers. Through a more unified and coordinated program for professional development, administrative team members can focus more effort to support teachers. If the members of the administrative team are not on the same page, mixed messages will be sent to teachers about the importance and value of professional growth, and credibility will diminish in the eyes of teachers.

The following discussion provides approaches for the principal to unify the efforts of the administrative team. As with the many suggested approaches and leadership tools presented in this book, the principal is encouraged to modify the following approaches to match the needs of the school.

Working with Administrative Team Members

Assistant Principals as Instructional Leaders

It is common for principals to assume that they bear the weight of being *the* instructional leader and for assistant principals to assume such tasks as managing discipline, athletics, facilities, and activities. Although these are critical tasks deserving of attention, assistant principals typically have a narrow job description that *restricts* them from emerging as instructional leaders (Marshall, 1992; Weller & Weller, 2001). When assistant principals become overidentified as gatekeepers and managers of noninstructional areas, boundaries are created. Unfortunately, teachers, who do not have an affiliation with these areas find little reason to interact with assistant principals.

Because of the frenetic work world of the assistant principal, who assumes multiple duties and responsibilities, there is traditionally little built-in time for learning about and then assuming a stronger instructional leadership position or status within the school. It is important for the principal to begin thinking of ways for assistant principals to emerge as instructional leaders. One way to do this is to determine their interests (e.g., mentoring, coaching, study group facilitation) and then "let them loose" to work with teachers and the instructional program.

Another strategy is to provide opportunities for assistant principals to participate in staff development related to instructional leadership skills. Staff development and ongoing learning is as important to assistant principals as it is to teachers. Just because an assistant principal has an interest in a topic does not mean that she has the expertise, knowledge, and training to design a program. However, with some training and coaching, these skills can be developed.

New Instructional Leadership Roles for the Administrative Team

Examining the structure of the administrative team begins with an open exploration of the values and beliefs about teaching and learning within the team. From uncovering these values and beliefs, the principal will be in a better position to lead the team into developing a vision for professional development.

To unify the members of the administrative team, the proactive principal provides ongoing opportunities for discussion about their core beliefs about supervision, staff development, and adult learning. Before beginning this exploration, the principal prepares by identifying the instructional needs of teachers based on initiatives at the site (e.g., school improvement plan), across the district, or changes within the school (e.g., a new curriculum or modification of the structure of the school day).

By having a ballpark indication of these needs, the principal can better

- ◆ forecast the types of resources needed to meet needs;
- ◆ ensure alignment in meeting both the needs of the system and its people;
- ◆ match the interests of the administrative team with needs; and
- ◆ determine what types of staff development members of the administrative team need so they can prepare to work in more proactive ways with teachers.

As the administrative team defines their role in professional development, a more unified, systematic, and coherent plan can emerge to better use the strengths of the administrative team. The talk over time by the members of the administrative team can serve as a compass for ongoing learning.

Uncover Core Values and Beliefs about Professional Growth

To assist the principal, the following questions are offered with encouragement to modify based on the context of the school.

- ♦ What do you believe, given our current situation, you can contribute to adult learning needs?

- ♦ What do you believe teachers want from professional development?

- ♦ When teachers feel good about teaching, what is occurring in classrooms?

- ♦ What aspects of your current position do you think add to promoting professional growth for teachers? For yourself?

- ♦ What types of support do you think our teachers need? From these support needs, which ones do you feel you can provide?

- ♦ Given your current duties and responsibilities, how can you "plug in" to an interest you have in professional development to meet a need of the school?

- ♦ What will get in your way? How can the team help by restructuring areas of responsibility and duty?

- ♦ What staff development do you need as an administrator to assist teachers ?

As these discussions continue, the principal will be in a solid position to assist the team in not only developing a vision for professional development but also a plan to bring the vision to fruition. As a result, the principal will be able to match the talents and interests of the administrative team to the needs of the school. The reader should review Chapter 2 for a detailed discussion on developing a vision.

Staff Development for Administrative Team Members

Staff development for the administrative team needs to build capacity within the individual so that they can

- ♦ develop instructional leadership skills;

♦ be involved in activities that promote ongoing development and refinement of instructional leadership skills;

♦ develop the motivation to take calculated risks by experimenting with leadership practices and procedures; and

♦ increase professional awareness and predict what types of support are needed to meet their needs and the needs of others.

Practices to Unify the Efforts of the Administrative Team

The principal is encouraged to examine Figure 3.2, Unifying Instructional Supervision, Staff Development, and Teacher Evaluation (p. 61). This model illustrates the interconnected nature of professional growth for adults by purposefully linking such activities as goal setting, multiple informal and formal classroom observations, staff development, and supervisory initiatives such as action research, peer coaching, and evaluation. The power of this model comes from the scaffolding of learning and the application of newly learned or refined information across each one of these processes. Coherence is also a prerequisite for unifying the efforts of the administrative team as they work with teachers. Changes in administrative practices can only survive if the principal, along with the members of the administrative team, are able to

♦ *Redefine relationships with each other and with teachers.* This redefining process begins with the principal flattening hierarchical structures found within leadership teams (e.g., principal, associate principal, assistant principal, deans, instructional deans, department chairs, lead teachers, and grade-level coordinators).

♦ *Share responsibility for learning.* All need to assume an active role in providing learning opportunities for themselves as they work with teachers.

♦ *Create an atmosphere of interdependence.* Each member of the team needs to feel a sense of belonging by being able to contribute to individual and collective learning opportunities while working alongside fellow administrative team members and teachers.

♦ *Make time for professional development.* Time is often cited as the main reason why principals and other members of the administrative team cannot function as instructional leaders. Consider your reaction if a teacher indicated that she did not have time to make it to class or to correct student work.

♦ *Develop a plan for professional development with teacher needs guiding the process.* No plan, if it is not grounded in the needs of its learners, will yield significant results.

♦ *Rotate responsibilities.* Rotation of specific duties and responsibilities associated with professional development can assist in getting all members of the administrative team on the same proverbial page. This rotation can also assist with breaking down barriers between people within the organization while supporting the development of skills and expertise across members of the administrative team.

♦ *Link schoolwide initiatives.* The coordination of initiatives will reduce unnecessary duplication of programs and provide resources to support initiatives.

These suggestions, if implemented and frequently monitored by the members of the administrative team, can create the conditions necessary to make learning the fabric of professional growth. The organization will become seamless as the base of leadership multiplies.

Summary

Being an instructional leader necessitates the steadfast action of the principal to provide the conditions for members of the administrative team to grow as they assume expanded responsibilities as instructional leaders. Supervision and staff development will remain a relatively uneventful spectator sport for administrative team members unless they are readied to assume new professional roles within the school community. This readiness begins by examining core beliefs about supervision, staff development, and adult learning. Readiness is translated into practice for administrative team members when staff development opportunities are provided for them. The members of the administrative team must strengthen their own leadership skills if the principal expects leading to transform teaching. It falls to the principal to get things right.

References

Acheson, K. A., & Gall, M. D. (1997). Techniques in the clinical supervision of *teachers: Preservice and inservice applications* (4th ed.). White Plains, NY: Longman.

Allen, T. (2001). The taxonomy of educational objectives. Retrieved December 27, 2001, from http://www.humboldt.edu/~tha1/bloomtax.html.

Barth, R. S. (2001a). *Learning by heart*. San Francisco, CA: Jossey-Bass.

Barth, R. S. (2001b). Teacher leader. *Phi Delta Kappan, 82*(6), 443–449.

Barton, L. G. (1989). *Quick flip questions for critical thinking: Bloom's taxonomy*. Toledo, OH: Winston.

Bellon, J. J., & Bellon, E. C. (1982). *Classroom supervision and instructional improvement: A synergetic process* (2nd ed.). Dubuque, IA: Kendall/Hunt Publishing Company.

Bloom, B. S. (Ed.) (1956) *Taxonomy of educational objectives: The classification of educational goals*. New York: Longman.

Bloom's Taxonomy [Counseling Services, University of Victoria] Retrieved December 27, 2001, from http://www.coun.uvic.ca/learn/program/ hndouts/bloom.html

Blumberg, A. (1980). *Supervisors and teachers: A private cold war* (2nd ed.). Berkeley, CA: McCutchan Publishing Corporation.

Brookfield, S. D. (1986). *Understanding and facilitating adult learning: A comprehensive analysis of principles and effective practices*. San Francisco, CA: Jossey-Bass.

Brookfield, S. D. (1995). *Becoming a critically reflective teacher*. San Francisco, CA: Jossey-Bass.

Bryk, A. S., & Schneider, B. (2002). *Trust in schools: A core resource for improvement*. New York: Russell Sage.

Burden, P. (1982, January). *Developmental supervision: Reducing teacher stress at Different career stages*. Paper presented at the Association of Teacher Educators National Conference, Phoenix, AZ.

Burke, P. J., Christensen, J. C., & Fessler, R. (1984). *Teacher career stages: Implications for staff development*. Bloomington, IN: Phi Delta Kappa Educational Foundation Whole No. 214.

Calabrese, R. L. (2002). *The leadership assignment: Creating change*. Boston, MA: Allyn and Bacon.

Calabrese, R. L., & Zepeda, S. J. (1997). *The reflective supervisor*. Larchmont, NY: Eye on Education.

Calabrese, R. L., Short, G., & Zepeda, S. J. (1996). *Hands-on leadership tools for principals*. Larchmont, NY: Eye on Education.

Chance, P. L., & Chance, E. W. (2002). *Introduction to educational leadership and organizational behavior: Theory into practice*. Larchmont, NY: Eye on Education.

Chenoweth, T. G., & Everhart, R. B. (2002). Navigating comprehensive school change: A guide for the perplexed. Larchmont, NY: Eye on Education.

Christensen, J., Burke, P. J., Fessler, R., & Hagstrom, D. (1983). *Stages of teachers' careers: Implications for professional development.* Washington, DC: National Institute of Education (ERIC Document Reproduction Services No. ED 227 054).

Cogan, M. (1973). *Clinical supervision.* Boston, MA: Houghton-Mifflin Company.

Conley, D. T. (1996). *Are you ready to restructure? A guidebook for educators, parents, and community members.* Thousand Oaks, CA: Corwin Press.

Conner, D. R. (1993). *Managing at the speed of change: How resilient managers succeed and prosper where others fail.* New York: Villard Books.

Costa, A. L., & Garmston, R. J. (1994). *Cognitive coaching: A foundation for renaissance schools.* Norwood, MA: Christopher-Gordon.

Council of Chief State School Officers. (1996). *Interstate school leaders licensure consortium standards for school leaders.* Washington, DC: Council of Chief State School Officers: Author.

Covey, S. R. (1990). *Principle-centered leadership.* New York: Simon & Schuster.

Crow, G. M., Matthews, L. J., & McCleary, L. E. (1996). *Leadership: A relevant and realistic role for principals.* Larchmont, NY: Eye on Education.

Dassel-Cokato Middle School. School Vision and Mission Statement. Cokato, MN: Retrieved October 1, 2002, from http://www.dc.k12.mn.us/MSCHOOL/Default.htm.

Deal, T. E., & Peterson, K. D. (1999). *Shaping school culture: The heart of leadership.* San Francisco, CA: Jossey-Bass.

Deal, T., & Peterson, K. (1993). Strategies for building school cultures: Principals as symbolic leaders. In M. Sashkin & H. J. Walberg (Eds.), *Educational leadership and school culture* (pp. 89–99). Berkeley, CA: McCutchan.

De Bevoise, W. (1984). Synthesis of research on the principal as instructional leader. *Educational Leadership, 41*(5), 14–20.

Dewey, J. (1929). *Sources of science education.* New York: Liverisht.

Distance Learning Resources Network (DLRN). Technology Resource Guide. Chapter 4: Bloom's Taxonomy. Retrieved December 27, 2001, from http://www.dlrn.org/library/dl/guide4.html.

Dyer, W. G. (1995). *Team building: Current issues and new alternatives* (3rd ed.). Reading, MA: Addison-Wesley Publishing Company.

Edmonds, R. R. (1979). Effective schools for the urban poor. *Educational Leadership, 37*(1), 15–24.

Evans, R. (1996). *The human side of school change.* San Francisco, CA: Jossey-Bass.

Feiman, S., & Floden, R. (1980). *What's all this talk about teacher development?* East Lansing, MI: The Institute for Research on Teaching (ERIC Document Reproduction Service No. ED 189 088).

Fielder, D. J. (2003). *Achievement now! How to assure no child is left behind.* Larchmont, NY: Eye on Education.

Fiore, D. J. (2001). *Creating connections for better schools: How leaders enhance school culture.* Larchmont, NY: Eye on Education.

Fuhr, D. (1990). Supervising the marginal teacher: Here's how. *National Association of Elementary Teachers,9*(2), 1–4.

Fullan, M. (2001). *The new meaning of educational change* (3rd ed.). New York: Teachers College Press.

Fuller, F. (1969). Concerns of teachers: A developmental conceptualization. *American Educational Research Journal, 6*(2), 207–266.

Gagnon, G. W., & Collay, M. (2001). *Constructivist learning design.* Retrieved May 27, 2001, from http://www.prainbow.com/cld/cldp.html.

Glanz, J. (1998). *Action research: An educational leader's guide to school improvement.* Norwood, MA: Christopher-Gordon.

Glatthorn, A. A. (1990). *Supervisory leadership: Introduction to instructional supervision.* New York: HarperCollins.

Glatthorn. A. A. (1997). *Differentiated supervision* (2nd ed.). Alexandria, VA: Association for Supervision and Curriculum Development.

Glickman, C. D. (1981). *Developmental supervision: Alternative practices for helping teachers improve instruction.* Alexandria, VA: Association for Supervision and Curriculum Development.

Glickman, C. D. (1990). *Supervision of instruction: A development approach* (2nd ed.). Boston, MA: Allyn and Bacon.

Glickman, C. D., Gordon, S. P., & Ross-Gordon, J. M. (1998). *Supervision of instruction: A developmental approach.* (4th ed.). Needham Heights, MA: Allyn and Bacon.

Goldhammer, R. (1969). *Clinical supervision: Special methods for the supervision of teachers.* New York: Holt, Rinehart and Winston.

Goldhammer, R., Anderson, R., & Krajewski, R. (1993). *Clinical supervision: Special methods for the supervision of teachers* (3rd ed.). Fort Worth, TX: Harcourt Brace Jovanovich College.

Grady, M. P. (1998). *Qualitative and action research: A practitioner handbook.* Bloomington, IN: Phi Delta Kappa.

Guskey, T. R. (2001). *Evaluating professional development.* Newbury Park, CA: Corwin Press.

Hammonds, B. (2002). Quality learning. At leading-learning.co.nz. Retrieved November 16, 2002, from http://www.leading-learning.co.nz/school- vision/vision-process.html

Hargreaves, A. (1997). Cultures of teaching and educational change. In M. Fullan (Ed.), *The Challenge of School Change* (pp. 57–84). Arlington Heights IL: Skylight Training and Publishing.

Harris, B. M. (1975). *Supervisory behavior in education* (2nd ed.). Englewood Cliffs, NJ: Prentice Hall.

Harvey, T. R., & Drolet, B. (1994). *Building teams, building people: Expanding the fifth resource.* Lancaster, PA: Technomic Publishing.

Hirsh, S., & Ponder, G. (1991). New plots, new heroes in staff development. *Educational Leadership, 49*(3), 43–48.

Hong, L. K. (1996). *Surviving school reform: A year in the life of one school.* New York: Teachers College Press.

Hord, S. M., Rutherford, W. L., Huling-Austin, L., & Hall, G. E. (1987). *Taking charge of change.* Alexandria, VA: Association for Supervision and Curriculum Development. Hoy, A. W., & Hoy, W. K. (2003). Instructional leadership: A learning-centered guide. Boston, MA: Allyn & Bacon.

Huberman, M. (1993). (Jonathan Neufeld, Trans.) *The lives of teachers.* New York: Teachers College Press. (Original work published 1989).

Interstate School Leaders Licensure Consortium. (1996). *Standards for school leaders.* Retrieved July 7, 2001, from http://www.ccsso.org/standrds.html. Author.

Joyce, B., & Showers, B. (1982). The coaching of teaching. *Educational Leadership, 40*(2), 4–10.

Kallick, B. (1997). Measuring from in the middle of learning. In A. L. Costa & R. M. Lieberman (Eds.), *Supporting the spirit of learning: When process is content* (pp. 203–219). Thousand Oaks, CA: Corwin Press.

Katz, L. (1972). Developmental stages of preschool teachers. *Elementary School Journal, 73*(1), 50–54.

Katzenbach, J. R., & Smith, D. K. (1993). *The wisdom of teams: Creating the high performance organization.* Boston, MA: Harvard Business School Press.

Katzenmeyer, M., & Moller, G. (1996). *Awakening the sleeping giant: Leadership development for teachers.* Newbury Park, CA: Corwin Press.

Killion, J. (2001). *Assessing impact: Evaluating staff development.* Oxford, OH: National Staff Development Council.

Komives, S. R. (1994). New approaches to leadership. In J. Fried (Ed.), *Different voices: Gender and perspective in student affairs administration* (pp. 46–61). Washington, DC: National Association of Student Personnel Administrators.

Kouzes, J. M., & Posner, B. Z. (2001). *The leadership challenge: How to keep getting extraordinary things done in organizations* (3rd ed.). San Francisco, CA: Jossey-Bass.

Krug, S. E. (1992). Instructional leadership: A constructivist perspective. *Educational Administration Quarterly, 28*(3), 430–443.

Kruse, S., Louis, K. S., & Bryk, A. (1994). Building professional community in schools *Issues in restructuring Schools, 6,* 3–6. Madison, WI: Center on Organization and Restructuring of Schools, Wisconsin Center for Education Research, School of Education, University of Wisconsin-Madison.

Lambert, L. (1995). Toward a theory of constructivist leadership. In L. Lambert, D. Walker, D. P. Zimmerman, J. E. Cooper, M. D. Lambert, M. E. Gardner, & P. J. Slack (Eds.), *The Constructivist Leader* (pp. 28–51). New York: Teachers College Press.

Lane, B. A. (1992). Cultural leaders in effective schools: The builders and brokers of excellence. *NASSP Bulletin, 76*(541), 85–96.

Lawrence, C. E., Vachon, M. K., Leake, D. O., & Leake, B. H. (1993). *The marginal teacher: A step-by-step guide to fair procedures for identification and dismissal.* Newbury Park, CA: Corwin Press.

Leonard, L. J. (2002). Schools as professional communities: Addressing the collaborative challenge. *International Electronic Journal for Leadership in Learning, 6*(17). Retrieved September 9, 2002, from http://www.ucalgary.ca/~iejll/.

Lewin, K. (1936). Principles of topological psychology. New York: McGraw-Hill.

Lieberman, A., & Miller, L. (1999). *Teachers—Transforming their world and their work.* New York: Teachers College Press.

Lunenburg, F. C. (1995). *The principalship: Concepts and applications.* Englewood Cliffs, NJ: Merrill.

Lyons, A. A., & Pinnell, G. S. (2001). *Systems for change in literacy education: A guide to professional development.* Portsmouth, NH: Heinemann.

Maeroff, G. I. (1993). *Team building for school change: Equipping teachers for new roles.* New York: Teachers College Press.

Mallan Group Training and Management Inc. KnowMe™ Retrieved May 30, 2001, from http://www.knowmegame.com/Johari_Window/johari_ window. html.

Marshall, C. (1992). *The assistant principal: Leadership choices and challenges.* Thousand Oaks, CA: Corwin Press.

McBride, R., Reed, J., & Dollar, J. (1994). Teacher attitudes toward staff development: A symbolic relationship at best. *Journal of Staff Development, 15*(2), 36–41.

McGreal, T. (1983). *Effective teacher evaluation.* Alexandria, VA: Association for Supervision and Curriculum.

McNamara, C. (1999). Developing a Values Statement. Retrieved November 1, 2002, from http://www.mapnp.org/library/plan_dec/str_plan/stmnts. htm.

McQuarrie, F. O., & Wood, F. H. (1991). Supervision, staff development, and evaluation connections. *Theory in Practice, 30*(2), 91–96.

Mosher, R. L., & Purpel, D. E. (1972). *Supervision: The reluctant profession.* Boston, MA: Houghton-Mifflin Company.

Murphy, C. U., & Lick, D. W. (1998). *Whole faculty study groups: A powerful way to change schools and enhance learning.* Newbury Park, CA: Corwin Press.

Murphy, J. (1992). Effective schools: Legacy and future directions. In D. Reynolds & P. Cuttance (Eds.). School effectiveness: Research, policy, and practice (pp. 164–170). London: Cassell.

Murphy, J. (1994a). Transformational change and the evolving role of the principal: Early empirical evidence. In J. Murphy & K. S. Louis (Eds.), *Reshaping the principalship: Insights from transformational reform efforts* (pp. 20–53). Thousand Oaks, CA: Corwin Press.

Murphy, J. (1994b). *The reform of American public education: Perspectives and cases.* Berkeley, CA: McCutchan.

Nathan, J. (2002, November 17, 2002). Lack of mission hurting schools. [Education column]. *Pioneer Press on the Web.* Retrieved November 17, 2002, from http://www.twincities.com/mld/pioneerpress/living/education/ 4531724.htm

National Association of Elementary School Principals. (2001). *Leading learning communities: Standards for what principals should know and be able to do.* Alexandria, VA: National Association of Elementary School Principals: Author.

National Commission on Teaching and America's Future. (1996). *What matters most: Teaching for America's future.* New York: National Commission on Teaching and America's Future: Author.

National Foundation for Improving Education. (1996). *Teachers take charge of their learning: Transforming professional development for student success.* West Haven, CT: National Foundation for Improving Education Publications: Author.

National Staff Development Council. (n.d.).Standards for Staff Development. Retrieved January 15, 2003, from http://www.mdk12.org/instruction/leadership/staff_development/nsdc.html.

Newman, K., Burden, P., & Applegate, J. (1980). *Helping teachers examine their long-range development.* Washington, DC: Association of Teacher Educators (ERIC Document Reproduction Service No. ED 204 321).

Newman, K., Dornburg, B., Dubois, D., & Kranz, E. (1980). *Stress to teachers' mid-career transitions: A role for teacher education* (ERIC Document Reproduction Services No. ED 196 868).

Noddings, N. (1992). *The challenge to care in schools.* New York: Teachers College Press.

O'Neil, J. (1998). Constructivism—wanted: Deep understanding. In J. O'Neil & S. Willis (Eds.), *Transforming classroom practice* (pp. 49–70). Alexandria, VA: Association for Supervision and Curriculum Development.

Pajak, E. F. (1993). *Approaches to clinical supervision: Alternatives for improving instruction.* Norwood, MA: Christopher-Gordon.

Pascarelli, J. T., & Ponticell, J. A. (1994). Trust-blocking responses. Training Materials Developed for Co-Teaching. Chicago, IL.

Pasternak, B. A., & Viscio, A. J. (1998). *The centerless corporation: A new model for transforming your organization for growth and prosperity.* New York: Simon & Schuster.

Peter F. Drucker Foundation for Nonprofit Management. Drucker Foundation Self-Assessment Tool: Content How to Develop a Mission Statement. Retrieved November 16, 2002, from http://www.pfdf.org/leaderbooks/sat/mission.html

Peterson, K. D. (2000). *Teacher evaluation: A comprehensive guide to new directions and practices.* (2nd ed.). Thousand Oaks, CA: Corwin Press.

Peterson, K. D. (2002). Positive or negative? *Journal of Staff Development, 23*(3), 10–15.

Platt, A. D., Tripp, C. E., Ogden, W. R., & Fraser, R. G. (2000). *The skillful leader: Confronting mediocre teaching.* Acton, MA: Ready About Press.

Purkey, S. C., & Smith, M. S. (1983). Effective Schools: A review. *The Elementary School Journal, 83*(4), 427–452.

Robb, L. (2000). *Redefining staff development: A collaborative model for teachers and administrators.* Portsmouth, NH: Heinemann

Robbins, P., & Alvy, H. B. (1995). *The principal's companion: Strategies and hints to make the job easier.* Thousand Oaks, CA: Corwin Press.

Saphier, J., & King, M. (1985). Good seeds grow in strong cultures. *Educational Leadership, 42*(6), 67–74.

Sarason, S. B. (1995). *School change: The personal development of a personal point of view.* New York: Teachers College Press.

Sawa, R. (1995). Teacher Evaluation Policies and Practices Retrieved December 1, 2002, from http://www.ssta.sk.ca/research/instruction/95-04.htm

Schein, E. H. (1992). *Organizational culture and Leadership* (2nd ed.). San Francisco, CA: Jossey-Bass.

Schlechty, P. C. (1997). *Inventing better schools: An action plan for educational reform.* San Francisco, CA: Jossey-Bass.

Seikaly, L. H. (2002). Principal's role in creating a vision. School Improvement Maryland (MDK12). Retrieved November 16, 2002, from http://www.mdk12.org/process/leading/principals_role.html

Sergiovanni, T. J. (1987). *The principalship: A reflective practice perspective.* Newton, MA: Allyn & Bacon.

Sergiovanni, T. J. (1994). *Building community in schools.* San Francisco, CA: Jossey-Bass.

Sergiovanni, T. J. (1995). *Leadership for the schoolhouse.* San Francisco, CA: Jossey-Bass.

Sergiovanni, T. J., & Starratt, R. J. (1998). *Supervision: A re-definition* (6th ed.). Boston, MA: McGraw-Hill.

Short, R., & Greer, J. (1997). *Leadership for Empowered Schools.* Columbus, OH: Merrill.

Showers, B., & Joyce, B. (1996). The evolution of peer coaching. *Educational* Leadership, *53*(6), 12–16.

Sparks, D., & Hirsh, S. (1997). *A new vision for staff development.* Oxford, OH: National Staff Development Council.

Speck, M. (1999). *The principalship: Building a learning community.* Upper Saddle River, NJ: Prentice Hall.

Stolp, S., & Smith, S. C. (1995). *Transforming school culture: Stories, symbols, values, and the leader's role.* Eugene, OR: ERIC Clearinghouse on Educational Management, University of Oregon.

Sullivan, S., & Glanz, J. (2000). Alternative approaches to supervision: Cases from the field. *Journal of Curriculum and Supervision, 15*(3), 212–235.

Team Management Systems © Prado Systems Limited (1993, 2002). The concepts: Types of work. Retrieved September 21, 2002, from http://www.tms.com.au/tms06.html.

Thompson, D. P. (1996). *Motivating others: Creating the conditions.* Larchmont, NY: Eye on Education.

Tirozzi, G. N. (2001). The artistry of leadership: The evolving role of the secondary school principal. *Phi Delta Kappan, 82*(6), 434–439.

U.S. Department of Education (1995). Building bridges: The mission and principles of professional development: Author. Retrieved October 13, 2002, from http://www.ed.gov/G2K/bridge.html

U.S. Department of Education (1999). Perspectives on Education Policy Research—Policy Brief: Effective Leaders for Today's Schools: Synthesis of a Policy Forum on Educational Leadership. Jessup, MD: U.S. Department of Education, Education Publications Center: Author. Retrieved October 18, 2002, from http://www.ed.gov/pubs/EffectiveLeaders/effective-leadership. html.

Vygotsky, L. (1978). *Mind in society: The development of higher psychological processes.* Boston, MA: Harvard University Press.

Waite, D. (1995). *Rethinking instructional supervision: Notes on its language and culture.* London, UK: Falmer Press.

Weller, L. D., & Weller, S. J. (2001). *The assistant principal: Essentials for effective school leadership.* Thousand Oaks, CA: Corwin Press.

Westheimer, J. (1998*). Among school teachers: Community autonomy and ideology in teachers' work.* New York: Teachers College Press.

Wheatley, M. (n.d.) Life affirming leaders. From the four directions: People everywhere leading the way. Retrieved November 9, 2002, from http://www.fromthefourdirections.org/tpl/ourarticles.tpl.

Wiles, J., & Bondi, J. (1996). *Supervision: A guide to practice.* Columbus, OH: Merrill.

Wisconsin Department of Public Instruction (2002). Characteristics of Successful Schools—Leadership. (2002). Retrieved October 8, 2002, from http://www.dpi.state.wi.us/dpi/dlsea/sit/cssldrshp1.html

Wood, F. H., & Killian, J. (1998). Job-embedded learning makes the difference in school improvement. *Journal of Staff Development, 19*(1), 52–54.

Yukl, G. (1994). *Leadership in organizations* (3rd ed.). Englewood Cliffs, NJ: Prentice Hall.

Zepeda, S. J. (1995). How to ensure positive responses in classroom observations. *Tips for Principals: National Association of Secondary School Principals.* Reston, VA: National Association of Secondary School Principals.

Zepeda, S. J. (1999). *Staff development: Building learning communities.* Larchmont, NY: Eye on Education.

Zepeda, S. J. (2003). *Instructional supervision: Applying tools and concepts.* Larchmont, NY: Eye on Education.

Zepeda, S. J., & Mayers, R. S. (2000). *Supervision and staff development in the block.* Larchmont, NY: Eye on Education.

Zepeda, S. J., Mayers, R. S., & Benson, B. N. (2003). *The call to teacher leadership.* Larchmont, NY: Eye on Education.